TOPSAIL ISLAND

Mayberry by the Sea

TOPSAIL ISLAND

Mayberry by the Sea

RAY McALLISTER

JOHN F. BLAIR
PUBLISHER

Excerpts from the interview of Caronell Chestnut by Dianne Adjan Logan, February 1995, are used with the permission of CreatiVideo, Inc., Wilmington, North Carolina.

Excerpts from *Norrh Carolina's Hurricane History*, copyright 2001, are reprinted with the permission of the University of North Carolina Press, Chapel Hill, North Carolina.

The "Stranded," "Vacation Wasteland," and "Here on an Island" lyrics are reproduced with the permission of Waterline Music, North Topsail Beach, North Carolina.

"Topsail Treasure Hunters Seek to Solve 300-Year-Old Mystery," from the *Wilmington News*, May 21, 1939, is reprinted with the permission of the *Star-News*, Wilmington, North Carolina.

*All photographs, including the cover,
are by Vicki McAllister except as noted.
Map by Roy Wilhelm
Design and composition by The Roberts Group*

Library of Congress Cataloging in Publication Data

McAllister, Ray, 1952-
  Topsail Island : Mayberry by the sea / by Ray McAllister.
    p.   cm.
  Includes bibliographical references and index.
  ISBN-13: 978-0-89587-331-6 (hardcover : alk. paper)
  ISBN-10: 0-89587-331-1 (hardcover : alk. paper)
  ISBN-13: 978-0-89587-330-9 (pbk. : alk. paper)
  ISBN-10: 0-89587-330-3 (pbk. : alk. paper)
  1. Topsail Island (N.C.)—History—Anecdotes. 2. Topsail Island (N.C.)—Social life and customs—Anecdotes. 3. Topsail Island (N.C.)—Biography—Anecdotes. 4. Interviews—North Carolina—Topsail Island. I. Title.

  F262.O5M33 2006
  975.6'23—dc22

                                    2006012579

For Mother and Dad

Contents

Preface   ix

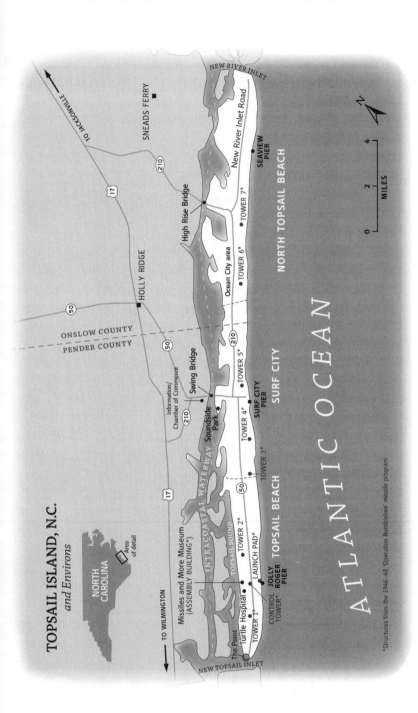

TOPSAIL ISLAND, N.C.
and Environs

NORTH CAROLINA

Area
of detail

TO WILMINGTON

TO JACKSONVILLE

SNEADS FERRY

17

210

210

HOLLY RIDGE

50

50

ONSLOW COUNTY

PENDER COUNTY

17

NEW RIVER INLET

New River Inlet Road

SEAVIEW
PIER

TOWER 7*

High Rise Bridge

Ocean City area

TOWER 6*

NORTH TOPSAIL BEACH

210

TOWER 5*

Swing Bridge

Information/
Chamber of Commerce

210

SURF CITY
PIER

SURF CITY

Soundside
Park

TOWER 4*

INTRACOASTAL WATERWAY

TOWER 3*

50

TOPSAIL BEACH

Missiles and More Museum
(ASSEMBLY BUILDING*)

TOPSAIL SOUND

TOWER 2*

LAUNCH PAD*

JOLLY
ROGER
PIER

CONTROL
TOWER*

TOWER 1*

Turtle Hospital

The Point

NEW TOPSAIL INLET

ATLANTIC OCEAN

N

0   2   4
MILES

*Structures from the 1946–48 "Operation Bumblebee" missile program

Preface

W*hen first I saw Topsail Island, it looked like the surface of the moon.* The year was 1996, and Hurricanes Bertha and Fran had just hit. Fran, especially, had been unkind.

My parents lived in Wilmington, North Carolina, about a 45-minute drive away. My father, a semi-retired insurance inspector, took my family up to view some of what he had seen. What he had seen was devastation: buildings knocked down, beaches eroded, homes tossed about as if they were Pick-up Sticks. We drove through the new town of North Topsail Beach, hardest hit, now more beach than town. Virtually nothing stood. Most of the damaged homes had been bulldozed. Piles of building materials remained to be carried away. Many piles had been cleared already.

Growing up, I had seen ghost towns in Arizona—entire communities left empty when a mine ran out. Street after street of houses remained, but each home was empty. With no buyers available, the occupants had simply left. In a sense, Topsail seemed even more surreal. A town had been here, clearly, but little more could be seen. When we could drive no farther, blocked by blown sand, we got out of the car and walked. The outlines of streets were visible, but the streets themselves were hidden. It was as if a tarp of sand had been draped over the island. Mother Nature had reclaimed what was hers.

I was not to see Topsail for nine more years. Our oldest daughter, Lindsay, her husband, Micah, and their newborn daughter, Riley, visited while returning from my parents' in the summer of 2004. They stopped at Topsail Beach, stayed in a motel, loved the island, and persuaded all of us to return the following summer.

In August 2005, then, we all returned—Vicki and I; Lindsay, Micah, and Riley; our son Ryan; our youngest daughter, Jamie, and Jamie's boyfriend. Behind our rental house were inland waters off the Intracoastal Waterway, which parallels the ocean. Off to the east—and we could see this from the same second-story deck—was the ocean.

The north end of the island had been rebuilt by now. But it was the island's calm and serenity, not the continual building, that we found striking. The waves and the breeze. A beautiful beach of white sand. The casual pace. Friendly people. Small shops. We found a breakfast place. Lindsay and Micah had discovered it the year before.

Topsail reminded me of visits years ago to my grandparents' home on Brigantine, New Jersey, a quaint island north of Atlantic City—quaint until gambling moved into Atlantic City and the moneyed crowds moved to Brigantine. It reminded me, too, of Nags Head on North Carolina's Outer Banks, which I visited years later with a college girlfriend's family. Nags Head had been small and slow paced and unassuming, not yet discovered by hordes of tourists, developers, and businesses. But Nags Head, like Brigantine, was all in the past now. There was no place like that anymore.

Yet here was Topsail. I went home and wrote about it. I write a column for the *Richmond Times-Dispatch*, and the response to this column was unusual. I received dozens of e-mails, calls, and letters, odd in themselves for a column about a mere place and not an issue or person. Many were from Virginia, of course, but a good many were from Topsail or elsewhere in North Carolina. Second, nearly everyone said I had perfectly described the allure of Topsail—not a particularly difficult task, I remember thinking. How tough is it to describe a paradise? Many with a history at Topsail told me their own stories. Finally, and I initially thought this was just hyperbole until the examples began to pile up, several politely asked me to write no more about Topsail. They begged me not to let the cat out of the bag.

The cat, I was pretty sure, had long since escaped. Everywhere we had gone on Topsail, houses and duplexes were being built. So I was taken by the notion that Topsail needed to be written about, and soon, while it was still Topsail. During the week at the beach, I had gone looking for a book to describe the allure of Topsail. I wanted something to read in a few days on the beach. I found a solid history of the island, but I was looking for something that would tell me why I liked this place. Now, readers were telling me the same thing. They wanted that book.

Among the many who e-mailed me was the head of the chamber of commerce for the Topsail area. A few back-and-forth exchanges led to my planning return trips to the island—one more in the summer and three in the fall and early winter. He lined up contacts, who in turn lined up others, who in turn lined up others. I also interviewed some of my original readers in Virginia.

In the end, I talked to more than 50 people—many of whom Vicki photographed for this book—before simply cutting things off. One or two islanders had to warm to the idea of talking to me, seemingly seeing me, I thought, as Native Americans once viewed soul-stealing photographers. I was after the island's soul, it was true, but I certainly meant it no harm. Of those 50-plus people, all but two ended up being warm, engaging, and sharing. That would prove typical of the island. Where else would you get a 96 percent helpfulness ratio?

In the end, this became a book of my observations, steered by the stories of others.

It is not a history book. Island history comes in through the side door, not the front door. Topsail, for instance, has a significant military history that is dispensed with quickly here. The interested reader would do well to check the books of local historian David A. Stallman.

And it is not a book of stories either. The stories within these pages are good ones, but more important is what they convey of the island's life. The selection of stories, I should say, was a combination of happenstance and arbitrary decision making. I can't help thinking that many will read this book and wonder what elevated these stories above their own. Everybody will believe he or she has stories that are just as good and just as meaningful and maybe more deserving. They're right. That's one of the wonderful things about living on Topsail Island.

Throughout the planning, researching, and writing of this book, I have always kept one question in mind: What is the allure of Topsail?

I hope you feel the answer.

CHAPTER ONE

Mayberry by the Sea

Sunsets on Topsail Island are worth the *wait*. The sun moves deliberately, as everything does on the island, reaching for the water of the sound but in no particular hurry to get there. A boat motors by. Sea gulls cry.

The sunlight begins to fracture as it nears the water, more so if the day is cloudy. Yellows and oranges extend through the sky, slowly at first, then rapidly filling the horizon. The blue-green water, initially a counterpoint, now catches fire from the sky, merging into a full-screen panorama of orange. An onlooker has to squint. All is brightness, beauty, color.

Moments later, it is gone.

Blackness nearly consumes the sky now,

interrupted by only a white-yellow moon. Across the narrow island, just a few hundred yards away, nature has prepared an encore. The fortunate need walk only a half-dozen blocks from Topsail Sound along the narrow streets thinly dusted by sand, up and over the decking that crosses the protective dunes, then down the steps. The view is to the east now, over the Atlantic Ocean. Moonlight bathes the beach and the incoming surf. Waves form, merge with one another, and roll toward the beach. Each momentarily commands the moon's spotlight as its fate is determined, either reaching the shore or being submerged by returning waves that have already made the journey.

Enough waves survive that their crashes on the beach are in rhythm every few seconds, the concussive downbeats to a tune played out by the sea.

An ocean breeze accompanies.

The sea mist joins in.

The enrapturing soft breeze, the ever-so-slight mist, the rhythmic sounds of the surf—they combine to wrap you in something so distinctive that when you experience a similar feeling days or weeks or even months later, in another place, perhaps on another beach, you will think of Topsail.

Topsail Island is a small barrier island off the North Carolina coast south of the Outer Banks and north of Wilmington and Wrightsville Beach. The map shows Topsail—pronounced "TOP-sul" by those who have been here more than once—to be pencil thin. Indeed, it is not much more. There are only 15 square miles on this 26-mile-long strip of sand. The width is rarely much more than a half-mile and sometimes only 200 yards, providing a splendor of almost incomprehensible logistics: morning sunrises over water followed, nearby, by evening sunsets over water. Did the Great Island Creator make a mistake? Was Topsail supposed to get both?

The map also shows Topsail divided among three towns: Topsail Beach at the south, Surf City in the middle, and the newcomer, North Topsail Beach, above them. The relative few residents who live on the island year-round will tell you the three are very much distinctive, that sometimes the towns are at odds politically, one town snubbing another that seeks cooperation, though the snubs seem to be lessening, and that—here their voices drop almost to a whisper—somehow folks who live in the other two towns are, well, different. It is true, they insist, but they say it with a smile, as if describing a slightly daft aunt or a cousin you just can't help loving anyway.

Visitors do not see the distinctions among the towns—not at first, anyway—nor do they necessarily care. The island is intoxicating. So what does it matter? Everyone is friendly.

Small shop owners—and there are no other kind on Topsail—are supposed to be friendly. But why the requirement that the man you meet walking the other way will not only say hello but will stop to say it? Who has decreed that the woman in the grocery store, whether one of the tiny mom-and-pops on the island or a supermarket just off, will ask how you're doing as if she cares how you are doing?

Who does that anymore?

People search for a way to describe the allure of Topsail. Allan Libby, director of the island's chamber of commerce, calls it simply "The Magic." The Magic, he says, is whatever draws a person to the island. The Magic is different things to different people.

Doug Medlin, who moved with his family to Surf City in 1952, when the number of island families could be counted on one hand, or surely on two, has a ready answer. "I think the quaint family atmosphere," he says. "When you think of Myrtle Beach, you think of all the shows, the rides. This is just a great family atmosphere."

Family is a part of it, to be sure. Quaintness is a part of it, too.

But isn't it odd that so many describe what Topsail has by enumerating what it doesn't have?

The island is always spoken about in those terms. It has a family atmosphere, someone will tell you. Even teenagers like the island, they will say—and then immediately launch into a laundry list of the things a teen would want that the island does *not* have. There is no shopping mall, of course, or anything like it. The nearest movie theater, well, that's the better part of an hour away. And so forth.

What sort of place is this?

"It's like you're back in time, this island is," says Jeffrey Stewart Price, who moved to Topsail Beach to take over the Beach Shop and Grill before the summer of 2002. "It's not a Myrtle Beach. It's not commercialized. People like that. It's for families." Even at the height of the season, the island is not what any new arrivals would call crowded.

The island does seem caught in a time warp, not yet overtaken by the commercial development of Virginia Beach, Nags Head, Wrightsville Beach, or Myrtle Beach. Nor is it likely to be. Topsail now is what those resorts were decades ago, even a half-century ago, or perhaps what we only thought they once were. Call it "the Little Island That Time Forgot." Many do. The moniker is intended as more endearing than demeaning. Topsail has a small-town feel of beach shops and cafés, a slow pace, and residents who know one another, as their parents and grandparents knew one another. Throw in the sea breezes, dunes, sea oats, and sea gulls and you have a Mayberry by the Sea. More than one smitten visitor has called it that. You can't help feeling that the residents of the fictional North Carolina town in *The Andy Griffith Show* would recognize these islanders. Is it coincidence that Griffith himself has spent much of his life on the North Carolina coast, even keeping a home on Figure Eight Island, just south of Topsail?

Even the Topsail Island police departments, rarely troubled by serious crime, specialize in community relations, just as in the fictional town of . . . well, you know.

That step back in time is part of The Magic. So, too, is the ocean setting. The surf, the breeze, the mist. And the fishing. The surfing. The diving and even nearby parasailing, for those inclined. And no doubt the isolation factors in. You can't get here from there, they say. Sometimes, it seems you can't get here from anywhere, so maybe the difficulty of the journey is part of what makes the destination more rewarding.

But who is in a hurry?

No one, at least not for very long.

The main road down the narrow island—in places, there is room for only one road—rarely carries a speed limit of more than 45 miles an hour; often it is 35 and sometimes 25. And yet the speed limit seems too high. Most drivers go 10 miles an hour under the limit. Who goes 10 miles an hour *under* anymore? "Slow Down," reads one island bumper sticker. "This Ain't the Mainland." Indeed. Vacationers invariably find themselves riding the bumpers of the cars in front when they arrive. By the end of the week, they are the ones slowing down the next week's arrivals.

Garth Boyd is a "come-here" who understands The Magic. His business had nothing to do with the island—he was in the pork industry, after all, not the resort or fishing business. In 1994, he moved from Colorado to North Carolina to start a new job. His new home was an hour away from Topsail. But then he and his wife were invited to a party on the island. "We fell in love with it. It just had a great feel to it," he says. Lynette Boyd in particular was overtaken by The Magic. "My

Quaint beach cottages, uncrowded beaches, and old-fashioned
shops make a visit to the island feel like a step back in time.
Topsailians explain the island's small-town allure in similar terms.
"It's family-oriented," they may say, or "It's not Myrtle Beach." Nothing
against Myrtle Beach, mind you.

wife had the crazy idea that, why don't we buy a place at the
beach and *rent* where we are now?" That was backwards, of
course. People live elsewhere and rent their beach houses.

Nonetheless, they checked out an island house under construction. "We walked up on the deck right at sunset and high
tide," Garth Boyd remembers. "We were speechless. I had arrived in paradise. Sunset over the sound. A pride of dolphins
came swimming by." Boyd had traveled the world and lived in
the paradise that is Colorado. He has visited the *South Seas*,
for goodness' sake. And yet, he says, "I have never seen a
place so beautiful."

The seed was planted, and the Boyds found a nearby lot a
few weeks later. Within a year, they had a home built. More
than once, actually. Just three weeks after the home was
finished, Hurricane Fran brought four and a half feet of water into it, requiring substantial repairs to the bottom level,

though leaving undisturbed the living area on the upper two floors. Boyd was only 38 and working far from the island, yet he, his wife, and their four children began living in the home during weekends, holidays, and summers. Six years later, in 2002, the Boyds moved in full-time. Their home sits on the Topsail Sound side of the island, surrounded by gnarly oaks of the maritime forest. Boyd can jump in a boat and in 10 minutes be on the ocean side of the island, where the water is warm seven months a year. He often visits nearby uninhabited Lea Island, which he says is "spectacular, pristine, the way I assume it was 500 years ago."

Beyond the physical beauty, or perhaps because of it, Topsail Island has a slow pace. It is no place for clock watchers. Getting things done can be difficult. People do not seem constrained by time. RSVPs are not always answered. Appointments are not always kept. What can be done today can still be done tomorrow.

Boyd is charmed by Topsail's pace. "It's such a relaxing place." The island is full of small groups of people brought together by a location or an interest or a lifestyle, he says. "I hear numerous people: 'It's like a little Mayberry.' It is. We do leave our keys in the car. We leave the house unlocked. It definitely has a small-town feel, people walking and riding bicycles on the pedestrian path, stopping to talk to other people."

The Boyds have found The Magic. "It's the tranquility," Garth Boyd begins, before adding a list of what else it is: "It's Mother Nature bombarding your senses so many times. The tides. The beautiful blue water. Dolphins swimming by. Pelicans. We have an osprey nest nearby." Through the years, his children have seen the cycle of ospreys being born, maturing, then leaving the nest.

There is no escaping the daylong sensual bombardment.

"We get great sunrises over the ocean," Boyd says, "and incomparable sunsets over the sound."

The end of the day on Topsail is always worth the wait.

CHAPTER TWO

Early Days ...
and Pirates!

Topsail Island has an unusually romantic history, ably boosted by legend.

Human history on the island goes back as far as 10,000 years ago, when prehistoric Indians laid out carefully planned villages in the area, according to *Topsail Island in a Seashell*, a pamphlet first published in 1987 by the Historical Society of Topsail Island.

In 1524, Giovanni da Verrazano, believed to be the first non-native to see the island, wrote in his journal, "I could congratulate myself on beholding land which had never before been seen by any European. . . . All the shore was shoal, but free from rocks and covered with sand. The country was flat." He did find Indians, dressed in skins and wearing garlands of feathers.

The Indian presence continued. The Tuscaroras visited on seasonal hunting and fishing trips in the 1700s. Like fishermen since, they found fish, clams, crabs, and oysters. In 1979, a 12-year-old boy gathering oysters, Travis James Batson, discovered the remains of a canoe in the marsh behind the island. Experts called it a dugout canoe of early-1700s vintage, most likely Algonquin-made. Batson donated his find to what was then the North Carolina Department of Natural Cultural Resources. It was loaned to Topsail Island's Missiles and More Museum in 1995.

During the Civil War, the Confederate Army benefited from saltworks set up on the island to turn seawater into salt, a necessary ingredient for preserving meat, fish, and crops. Later, farmers drove pigs across the shallow waterway near the current Surf City bridge to graze on the grasses.

There was fishing and not much else on the island before the military arrived in the 1930s. In a pair of lengthy articles in *The State* magazine in 1979, Lindsey Grant wrote about an uncle's mullet-fishing crew he had been part of as a seven-year-old for five weeks in the summer of 1934. He described the island:

THERE WAS A DESOLATE AND WILD BEAUTY ABOUT THOSE BARRIER ISLANDS. The Atlantic washed onto the long beach in straight lines. Behind the beach was a bluff where the sea had eroded the sand dunes. Behind the bluff, the dunes rose twenty feet or more and were tacked down with beach-growing vines and low shrubs. Farther back was a mixed stand of wild-planed pines, yaupon holly and other salt-tolerant plants; it was full of birds. Behind that, in turn, were the brackish marshes and waterways which separate the outer islands from the mainland.

The area has mostly been subdivided, since World War II, into rows of beach cottages, but it was a lonely place then. Just out of sight to the south there was another fishing crew. To the north, on the shore of the inlet, a reclusive entrepreneur named Leo Jenkins made a bare living running a general store which supplied the crew and the occasional passing sport fisherman or hunter.

No bridge to the island existed until the United States military moved in. During World War II, with Camp Davis nearby, the island was seized for military maneuvers and anti-aircraft exercises. A small but important program for women pilots, Women Airforce Service Pilots (the WASPs), was based here. After the war, Topsail became the top-secret site of the nation's new guided-missile testing program, Operation Bumblebee.

No aspect of Topsail's history has a greater hold on the imagination than . . .

Pirates!

North Carolina's coast was on the route of most pirates who sailed the Atlantic and the Caribbean from the 1630s until they were brought under control in the 1720s. The state was a particular haven, wrote Hugh F. Rankin in *Pirates of Colonial North Carolina*. While South Carolina had an excellent harbor in Charleston, North Carolina's shallow sounds and inlets were better suited for the thieves of the high seas. The colony's thinly scattered population further encouraged them. So did citizens who saw pirates as a source of revenue. Pirates brought in luxury items, after all, and no one questioned them too closely about their origin. State officials were more likely to support the thieves than to harass them. By 1700, Edmund Randolph, the surveyor general of customs in the American colonies and a one-man campaign to eliminate pirates, was sending reports to England noting that North Carolina had a reputation as "a place which receives pirates, runaways and illegal traders."

Among the many pirates were Charles Vane, who so alarmed Carolinians that an expedition was sent to capture him; Christopher Moody, who became captain of a pirate ship at age 23, plundering ships off the coast and cheating his crew of some of the loot; William Lewis, who subdued a slave ship off the coast and later set his English crew adrift in a small boat; and brutal ex-prizefighter William Fly, who captured several vessels off the coast before heading for New England waters.

A pirate's life was not likely to be long. Three of the above were hanged. The fourth, Lewis, was killed by the French members of his crew.

Two better-known pirates have become the stuff of North Carolina legend.

Stede Bonnet, "the Gentleman Pirate," was born to privilege and education but turned hardhearted enough to become the only pirate said to have made a prisoner walk the plank. He was a British Army major, then a wealthy sugarcane plantation owner in the West Indies. Though he had no real seamanship skills, he inexplicably turned to piracy. Neighbors said he suffered from a "Disorder of the Mind"; he actually bought his first ship, rather than stealing it. After taking ships in Charleston, Bonnet sought sanctuary in one of North Carolina's inlets. Later, he sailed to the Bay of Honduras and met up with Edward Teach.

Bonnet was not altogether welcomed by Teach, a notorious pirate who didn't relish working with an amateur. He made Bonnet a virtual prisoner on his ship under the guise of treating him the way a man of exalted background deserved. Their ships, Teach in control, took at least a dozen others before they set sail for North Carolina. There, Teach double-crossed Bonnet by putting out to sea with all the plunder, Bonnet's included. Bonnet would continue pirating, more brutally now that he had seen his mentor's example. Finally, in late 1718, the Gentleman Pirate was captured and hanged in Charleston.

No pirate plays a more prominent role in Topsail Island's lore than Edward Teach, sometimes called Ned Teach. His real name was more likely Edward Thatch, and more likely still Edward Drummond.

But he was better know as the notorious Blackbeard.

The pirate from Bristol, England, took the nickname to enhance his reputation of evil in the New World, where he terrorized the seas in 1717 and 1718. His men ruthlessly attacked merchant ships—many of them off North Carolina—stealing goods, killing some crew members in battle, taking others into Blackbeard's crew, or setting them adrift. Blackbeard was said to have defeated the *Scarborough*, a 30-gun warship of the British Navy sent to subdue him. He sent it scurrying into retreat.

Not only his deeds were frightening. Blackbeard's very appearance seemed to be that of the devil. Lindley S. Butler, writing in *Pirates, Privateers, and Rebel Raiders of the Carolina Coast*, noted that the popular perception of Blackbeard seemed based primarily on a book appearing just six years following his death in 1718. After nearly three centuries, Captain Charles Johnson's *A General History of the Pyrates* remains one of the most definitive accounts of the pirate. Butler wrote, "Captain Johnson may have done as much for Thatch's larger-than-life image as did the rogue himself, with vivid descriptions of his 'remarkably black ugly Beard' that consisted of a 'large Quantity of Hair, which like a frightful Meteor, covered his whole face.' "

From eyewitness accounts, Blackbeard was a tall man with a long beard. He reportedly carried three pairs of pistols and his cutlass into battles. For effect, he went so far as to place around his face long, slow-burning matches of the type used to light cannons. According to Johnson's 1724 description, "this Beard was black, which he suffered to grow of an extravagant Length; as to Breadth, it came up to his Eyes; he was accustomed to twist it with Ribbons, in small Tails . . . and turn them about his Ears: In Time of Action, he wore a sling over his Shoulders, with three Brace of Pistols, hanging in Holsters like Bandaliers; and stuck lighted Matches under his Hat, which appearing on each Side of his Face, his Eyes naturally looking fierce and wild, made him altogether such a Figure, that Imagination cannot form an Idea of a Fury, from Hell, to look more frightful."

Blackbeard haunted the sea lanes between the mainland and the West Indies. North Carolina, however, became his headquarters. The many inlets were perfect. For a while, the little town of Bath even served as Blackbeard's home—along with that of his 14th wife—as he lived in opulence with the acquiescence of the corrupt North Carolina governor. But his time was short. For the better part of two years, Blackbeard and his crew had terrorized the mid-Atlantic coast from Charleston to Pennsylvania, wrecking shipping and commerce. It was the Virginia governor, at the behest of North Carolinians who knew not to turn to their own governor, who sent a ship to take Blackbeard dead or alive.

Blackbeard, shown here in an engraving from a book appearing shortly after his death, terrorized the North Carolina coastline in 1717 and 1718. The notorious pirate may well have landed on Topsail, hidden behind the island to attack merchant ships, and even buried his treasure here. Then again, he may have done none of those things.

Blackbeard would be taken dead following a vicious fight at Ocracoke Inlet near the Outer Banks in November 1718. Butler called it "the bloodiest six minutes ever fought on Carolina waters." Blackbeard's throat was slashed, the fatal wound of the 25 on his body, five of which were delivered by pistol balls, according to Rankin. Still, his powerful body attempted to fight on. The pirate pulled another pistol from his belt and was beginning to cock it when he fell over dead on the deck. His head was severed from his body and later displayed on a stick in Virginia as a lesson to would-be pirates.

Within months of Blackbeard's death at Ocracoke, Butler wrote, a teenaged Benjamin Franklin was hawking the ballad

"A Sailor Song on the Taking of Teach or Blackbeard the Pirate" in the streets of Boston. The concluding stanza:

> *And when we no longer can strike a blow,*
> *Then fire the magazine, boys, and up we go!*
> *It's better to swim in the sea below*
> *Than to swing in the air and feed the crow,*
> *Says jolly Ned Teach of Bristol.*

Blackbeard's is a fascinating story—a terrorizing thief in his day, a romantic swashbuckler centuries later, always larger than life.

Legend has it that pirates, Blackbeard among them, would wait in the channel behind Topsail Island for passing merchants' ships. Behind the island's dunes and maritime forest, their ships could not be seen, other than the tips of the uppermost sails. Using the element of surprise, the pirates would speed around the island, run down passing ships, and take their goods—and sometimes the crews' lives. Eventually, the passing captains caught on and began to look for sail tips above the dunes. Given a head start, their merchant ships could maintain a safe distance.

But Blackbeard's legend goes still further on Topsail. Before his life was taken at Ocracoke, the story goes, Blackbeard buried his treasure on Topsail Island. All the wealth of history's most notorious pirate is available to anyone who can find it.

But did Blackbeard even visit Topsail?

Evelyn Bradshaw, one of the leading lights in the founding of the island's museum, thinks it's logical that he did. "Blackbeard sailed up and down the coast," she says. "It was a perfect place for him to have stopped." The island and its hiding places were hospitable to pirates. When she tells the story of

Blackbeard to schoolchildren, though, she is careful to call it a legend.

While the story is plausible, proof is scant.

Blackbeard certainly sailed past Topsail Island in his *Queen Anne's Revenge*, one time in particular after blockading Charleston for nearly a week before sailing north. Butler noted that "the pirate fleet worked slowly up the coast to North Carolina, seeking a place to careen their vessels," eventually reaching what is now Beaufort Inlet. So it is hardly impossible, nor even unlikely, that Blackbeard stopped at Topsail.

Bill Sharpe, writing in the *Wilmington News* of May 21, 1939, noted with only some hyperbole that Blackbeard "frequented the ancient towns of Bath, New Bern, Edenton and other maritime villages . . . and it is a poor town indeed in coastal North Carolina which cannot boast of a 'Blackbeard house.' " Indeed, Sharpe, in his four-volume *A New Geography of North Carolina*, published in the 1950s and 1960s, noted that stories exist about both Bonnet and Blackbeard at Topsail: "Legend says Bonnet hid his loot on the Pender [County] strand. Another says that Blackbeard looted two of Bonnet's ships in the sound."

The *Topsail Island in a Seashell* pamphlet made claims for both Blackbeard's presence and the naming of the island itself: "Topsail . . . got its name in the 1600s when 'the fiercest pirate of them all' Blackbeard tried to hide his ships in the wooded inlets of the island in an attempt to prey upon merchant ships as they sailed north laden with cargo from the West Indies. The ploy was a success only until the merchant captains learned to spot the highest masts, or Tops'ls, of the pirate ships, thus standing a chance of outrunning the dreaded looters."

They are romantic notions both, but the evidence is at best inconclusive.

How, then, did the legend gain such a foothold?

No doubt, some confusion lies in a name. Blackbeard chose Topsail Inlet to intentionally ground the *Queen Anne's Revenge* as part of an elaborate plan to keep the considerable booty he had taken, trim a too-large and somewhat mutinous crew, and apply for a gubernatorial pardon. A law professor at Wake Forest University, Robert E. Lee, offered this explanation in his 1974 book, *Blackbeard the Pirate: A Reappraisal of His Life and Times*: "On the pretense of careening his ships for the purpose of scraping their hulls, Blackbeard, in early June, 1718, ordered his entire fleet to sail into what was then known as Topsail Inlet on the coast of North Carolina. Today Topsail Inlet is commonly known as Beaufort Inlet and is the inlet used to reach the towns of Beaufort and Morehead City. It is not to be confused with the much smaller Topsail Inlet presently located about fifty or sixty miles to the south."

Not to be confused—but frequently confused nonetheless. One suspects that may be as much on purpose as not. Tourist brochures mention the Topsail "legend" of Blackbeard. Island attractions take his name for everything from a miniature golf course to a campground. The island itself is sometimes called "the Treasure Coast." Topsail stores eagerly sell pirate souvenirs. The Jolly Roger is one of the island's fishing piers. The town of Topsail Beach features a pirate ship in its logo.

And the legend of the pirates happily continues on Topsail.

Who can say it didn't happen?

CHAPTER THREE

The Gold Hole

*T*he May 21, 1939, issue of the Wilmington News—*a paper that later merged with the*
Morning News *to form the* Star-News—*greeted
readers with a fascinating story, one that would
in time come to be known as the greatest mystery
the island of Topsail has ever seen.*

It was a story of a long-lost Spanish galleon, a secret treasure map, the shifting sands
of Topsail, and a hugely expensive gold-ex-
ploration dig backed in part by the brother of
famed New York City mayor Jimmy Walker.
The dig would end up taking four years, from
1937 to 1941, and then simply end. Abruptly.
Mysteriously. All that was left was the Gold
Hole.

And questions.

That morning's story was accompanied by a photo of a huge hole looking like a construction site. It was captioned, "Going Down Into The Past." The caption identified "the big cofferdam ... which has been sunk in the sands of Topsail Beach over the wreck of an old ship. Workers have reached quicksand and are trying to remove it to get to the wreck, which lies 40 feet below water level. Considerable money already has been spent in the hunt."

The story was reported by the enterprising Bill Sharpe, who ventured out to a desolate island referred to then as Topsail Beach. The story is as enthralling and mysterious today as it was that Sunday morning in 1939:

TOPSAIL TREASURE HUNTERS HOPE TO SOLVE MYSTERY 300 YEARS OLD

"I may not get it, but it's there," said Julian S. Jacobs firmly. By "it" he meant an ancient ship, still 25 feet away from the top of the muck his crew is steadily reducing with a steam bucket. And in that ship, which mysteriously piled up on a wilderness reef perhaps 400 years ago, is gold and silver.

How much? If Jacobs knows he won't say. But there is a clue to this, too. The Carolina Exploration company of which Jacobs, a mining engineer from New York, is president, has been going after that ship for a year. Excavation work alone has cost between $15,000 and $20,000, according to local contractors, and Jacobs thinks his find—if and when he makes it—is going to return a handsome dividend on that investment, including a percentage of all treasure for Dr. William H. Walker, brother of former Mayor James J. Walker, of New York, who owns rights to the scientific instrument responsible for locating the booty. Another officer in the company is Harrison Gunnings, of Brooklyn. A third partner, Louis H. Hepp, died recently.

RELUCTANT TO TALK

Jacobs talked reluctantly of his treasure hunt, but his faith in the romantic quest shone through his reticence. The story back of the present operation, as he told it to a reporter sitting in his crude camp cabin housing his crew of diggers, while the surf roared nearby, is the story both of a hard-headed engineer and an incurable romanticist.

In the first place, Jacobs became interested in the scientific metal locator in connection with prospecting. His company operates several mines in North Carolina, and apparently his faith in the invention is based upon success in that field.

For the fun of it, as he says, Jacobs came to the Carolina banks to try out the instrument, hoping merely to pick up some old chest. But at Topsail Beach, a lonely strand a few miles off the North Carolina coast, north of Wrightsville Beach, he got a response that excited the crew of "chest" hunters. Down there somewhere, buried in the shifting sand, was a large mass of gold, silver and iron, according to the behavior of the "diviner" which operated on some unrevealed principle of radio-activity of elements.

The chest hunt was forgotten and the treasure hunters, after securing rights from owners of the beach, went to work, with the help of Edward J. Ives, salvage engineer of Hartford, Conn. The machine which located the metal has roughly outlined a ship, says Jacobs. . . . [T]hat part which should be the stern is the indication of gold and silver. Preliminary digging brought the treasure hunters to the water line. Now a huge cofferdam, with lock steel sheet piling, 45 feet long, has been sunk over the ship. The quicksand is being removed, but simply drilling indicates that the goal is 40 feet below the water line, and that means months more of work.

Not Discouraged

Nevertheless Jacobs and his crew are not discouraged. Every step downwards has seemed to confirm the accuracy of the treasure-finder. Pressure pumps have boiled up sand from the depths and have brought up bits of rotten wood which Jacobs says were obviously hand-tooled. How did it get there? On top of the site, the salvagers cleared off stumps of pine trees estimated to be 150 years old. Allowing any reasonable time for the ship to become "sanded up," the wreck must be between 300 and 400 years old.

Among the fisherfolk along the banks, it is popularly supposed that the treasure hunters got their first clue to the wreck from an old map, which, it is said, was discovered in London.

Jacobs denies this vigorously. Originally he came to Topsail because he knew it to be the custom of Blackbeard, Kidd and others to dodge into the many inlets of the banks with their loot. He guessed that when pirates slipped through into the quiet sound waters they could do their treasure burying at that time.

But the job itself has nothing to do with any such small matter. What the ship is, why it lies so deeply in the sand, the treasure hunters may only guess. There is no record of the shipwreck at that place, and the nearest inlet is about 7 miles away. Jacob offers a guess. He thinks that perhaps some vessel, respectable or illicit, loaded with gold and silver from Mexican mines, came into the channel during a storm and was wrecked upon the reef. It is well known that the banks of North Carolina are slowly moving toward the mainland. The old ship, then, was engulfed by the moving bar. At the point [where] the hunters are digging is a substantial dune, lending credence to the idea that sand has formed around some object.

Jacobs' absorption in his ship and its treasure is heightened by his curiosity about her identity. Was it a Spanish caravel, a slow freighter going home with treasure 400 years ago, when Mexico's mines were enriching the old country, only to come to grief on a yet-unexplored coast? Did he run away from pirates? Is she an English free-booter, bursting with stolen wealth? The treasure hunters hope that in that quicksand may lie answers to some of these questions—perhaps a brass plate or some other imperishable mark. One mystery probably will never be solved, however—the mystery of what became of the crew. They might have been lost in a storm, and the ship might have drifted up the channel from Topsail Inlet, even miles south. They might have taken to the boats and landed on the shore long before Raleigh's ill-fated colonists were swallowed by the same forests.

A Lonely Spot

The treasure hunt is being conducted on one of the loneliest strands. The only way to get there is to hire a boat and search the place out. The top of the excavating machine's derrick can be faintly discerned from the mainland. There is a crew of local workmen [who] labor in a little grove of wind-blown live oak and yaupon—a desolate but picturesque spot which would gladden the heart of a goldbug devotee except for the raucous evidence of civilization's methods of treasure hunting.

The fishermen nearby are divided on the chances of success. But one fisherman confidentially whispered that Jacobs and his crew were on the right track. He told this story:

"One day after a bad no'easter," he says, "the water swept away a big section of the beach and I caught my nets on part of an old wreck. I know the place well, because I marked it in my mind by a path which came down to the water. Well, sir, when these fellows came here with their doodle-bug thing, I took the mover in my boat. They found the wreck first—where they are working now. Then they went on down the path, and damned if they didn't stop right at the water's edge where I'd found that old wreck. The machine showed gold and silver in that, too, but they ain't telling anybody. It may be part of the same wreck. Anyways, that blamed machine took them right to the spot."

Treasure hunting is nothing new in North Carolina, and it has not always been attended by failure. . . .

Aside from buried treasure romanticism, the banks and sounds of North Carolina are a fertile field for the treasure hunter. The section was frequented by the most notorious and successful buccaneers of history, who found it an ideal hiding place and also found, at times, sympathetic officials willing to share in their loot. In addition to this, the shifting shoals trapped many an innocent ship, ancient and modern, with . . . more or less valuable cargoes. In the waters between Cape Hatteras and Diamond Lightship lie the wrecks of 200 ships, many of them in very shallow water. These are matters of record. And how many antique ships, beating northward from the Spanish Main, found grief on the shoals? No one knows. But Julian Jacobs thinks he has found at least one.

Was there a ship? If so, which ship? In a May 9, 1965, article entitled "Buried Treasure on the Tar Heel Coast" in the *Wilmington Morning Star*, writer Lewis Philip Hall laid out with seeming certainty a claim that it was a centuries-old treasure ship, part of a convoyed fleet blown off course: "[In] February 1750, a Spanish Flota of five vessels heavily loaded with treasure and the private cargo of the captain-generals of the fleet cleared from Veracruz following the usual defined route across the Gulf of Mexico." The ships, carrying precious metals and other treasures from the New World, reached Havana, then set sail again in late July, heading north in an effort to find favorable westerly breezes to take them home to Spain. But the late-summer winds became treacherous, Hall wrote: "About August 17, 1750, at some unknown point between Cape Fear and Cape Lookout on the North Carolina coast, the shrieking wind and mountainous seas of a full-fledged hurricane overtook and pounced on the high-pooped and helpless galleons. Under the terrific assault of towering waves and flying spume, which at times broke completely over the vessels, they staggered and heeled over, and in spite of the frantic efforts of the crew, were driven nearer and nearer the roaring surf and shoals."

Each of the five treasure ships ran aground on the North Carolina coast, though at different locations. Only one would be fit enough to resume its voyage. Hall, citing North Carolina's colonial records, said the first to run aground was the *El Salvadore* (or *El Henrico*). It probably went ashore "at New Topsail Inlet and was stove to pieces." Its cargo was gold, and it was loaded, the records say, "with 240,000 pieces of eight regular, besides what is on private account." It was that ship—the *El Salvadore*—for which the New York company was searching, Hall contended.

Was it? And was it ever found?

The mystery of the Gold Hole has become part of the island's lore, as mysterious and fuzzy around the edges as the stories of Blackbeard the Pirate.

Accounts surface from time to time, offering no answers beyond the speculative. Some 22 years after his 1939 visit to the site, Bill Sharpe, by then publisher of *The State* magazine, revisited the dig in volume 3 of his four-volume *A New Geography of North Carolina*. Sharpe said the treasure hunters had sunk the hole, which he then called the Old Spanish Galleon Pit, 50 feet or deeper. "No one knows if the diggers got anything. A five-foot steel casing still stands on the beach," he wrote. Sharpe distinguished the huge dig from a smaller one of 30 feet made farther inland on the Topsail Sound side. Likewise, though the diggers there found an old ship's timbers, "there is no evidence they got anything of value. Old residents call it the Old Pirate Ship Treasure Pit."

More recently, David A. Stallman, in writing his 1996 book, *Echoes of Topsail*, conducted personal interviews with two Topsail residents who worked on the Gold Hole but could confirm no find except some seemingly handcrafted wood. There were no answers beyond the abrupt end of the project in 1941, apparently caused by World War II.

The *Pender Chronicle* recounted the Gold Hole story in its June 30, 1965, edition, noting, "Many local residents were employed to assist with the digging and sinking of the steel shafts. Harvey Jones, owner of Harvey's Marina, can point out three places between the 'Dog-House' and the Dolphin Pier where shafts were sunk." But that newspaper came up with no answers either: "The Treasure?—no one will ever know. It is said that at the close of work one evening, the local men were laid off. The next morning the entire expedition was gone. Did they take with them the Treasure? It adds to the romance of the story to think of them stealthily hauling away chests of gold across the quiet waters of the sound—but no one seems to know."

Phil Mayrand was born five years after the Carolina Exploration company pulled out of Topsail. He, his sister Cecile Mayrand Broadhurst, and her husband, Ed, are the keepers of the Gold Hole and, by extension, the story. "My mother brought me here in 1946, when I was four months old," Mayrand says. The Gold Hole property, which belonged to the Bland family at the time of the dig, was part of a 66-foot-wide ocean-to-sound piece of land eventually bought by his parents, Louis and Evelyn Mayrand. Today, that property—in the town of Topsail Beach just south of the Surf City line—has passed to their children.

Phil Mayrand remembers being caught up in the story of gold. Legend had it that it was from Blackbeard's ship—a debatable point, but there were enough stories of pirate treasure being found up and down the East Coast to fire the imagination, Mayrand says. If it wasn't Blackbeard's, it was somebody's. "Every time I got out a shovel or a post-hole digger and would strike a root, I'd think, was that the treasure chest?" He laughs. "It's absolutely ridiculous," he admits. But it didn't seem that way at the time. As children, he and his friends did a lot of digging. "That was so soon after the Bumblebee [missile] program, we would find spent rockets." Anything seemed possible.

The expedition's digging apparatus was long gone, of course. But the Gold Hole was still squared off, 10 or 12 feet by a similar length, with lumber and steel holding the walls in place. "I remember as a child being able to find those little narrow rails for mining carts," Mayrand adds. But by that time, the Gold Hole served mainly as a draw for occasional curiosity seekers and as a local landfill. "My mother attempted to fill that hole up will all sorts of things I don't even want

Phil Mayrand, one of the owners of the Gold Hole property, played around the massive hole as a child and discovered the narrow rails on which mining carts were hauled away. The Gold Hole fueled everyone's imagination. "Every time I got out a shovel or a post-hole digger and would strike a root, I'd think, was that the treasure chest?" he says.

to describe," he says with a laugh. The hole never could be filled.

Now, it takes a hunt to even find the Gold Hole.

It sits in front and to the side of the Broadhurst home, not far from Mayrand's. A fence separates it from the Broadhurst driveway. More than that, trees, vines, and other growth keep away the curious. "Mother Nature has stabilized everything," Ed Broadhurst says. Broadhurst put in wooden bulkheads as well.

Years ago, the hole was cleared, Broadhurst says. It turned out to be nearly full of water. The island is barely above sea level, so water is near the surface almost everywhere. The property around the hole is high—Broadhurst says it's the fourth-highest property on the island. The reason? Dirt and sand from the Gold Hole dig elevated all the land around it. The amount removed was extraordinary. Most of the island gradually slopes up from the water's edge. Here, out back of the Broadhurst home, the elevation rises dramatically from Topsail Sound.

Getting near the Gold Hole is extraordinarily difficult now.

The journey—and though it is but a relative few feet, it is a journey—requires repellant, and lots of it. The Gold Hole may not have held Blackbeard's treasure, but it cornered the market on mosquitoes. They are on a visitor moments inside the fence. The slope down from the fence is steep, nearly too steep to walk. The undergrowth grabs at feet and legs almost immediately. Most visitors give up after only a few steps, content to crane their necks and look at what appears to be a round opening of some sort. It is so covered with vegetation it is hard to say for sure.

One thing for sure is that the Gold Hole will remain. Broadhurst and Mayrand are developing the large piece of land, intending to build a few more homes but keeping trees and other vegetation as intact as possible. Most likely, Mayrand says, they will cap the hole to keep animals and children away. Most likely, they'll also put up a marker to identify the famous spot.

So what is the truth of the Gold Hole?

No one knows what the organizers of the famous dig found—or didn't find—because they disappeared so suddenly, Mayrand says. He knew one of the local men, now dead, who worked on the Gold Hole. "I talked with Richard Sidley. He said that they were paid and treated well." But Sidley didn't know what happened either.

The Gold Hole today has been mostly reclaimed by Mother Nature and is covered with vegetation. Mosquitoes stand guard.

Mayrand's theory is that they just gave up. Two factors played a role, he thinks: the project's failure to find anything and the mounting expense.

Broadhurst says there are three possible conclusions: "Number 1, it was a scam. Number 2, they hit something and got the heck out of Dodge [with the loot]. Or Number 3, they just quit." His guess? "I have often thought it was a scam." Once the organizers got money from investors, he means, they pursued the dig long enough to make it appear legitimate and then quit, keeping the rest of the money. Then again, he says, "some people said they hit something. A lot of people thought it was pirate treasure."

Evelyn Bradshaw, a longtime neighbor of the Gold Hole, says, "I would like to believe it's a scam, if that makes it more interesting."

A friend of Bradshaw's, the late Jane Bland Watson, on whose family's property the Gold Hole was dug, had yet another theory. Watson said in a late-1990s interview, recorded as part of a youth-group project at the Emma Anderson Memorial Chapel, that the dig's leaders stayed in the family's fishing cottage. "We were of the understanding that if they found the gold, we would get a share of it. You can imagine how [many times] we had spent that money. We just knew we were going to be rich." When the organizers pulled out, what happened was anyone's guess. "I say they found the gold and took it with them," Watson said, laughing, "and we didn't get any of that." One thing they did get, Watson said, was a beautiful sandy beach behind the home on Topsail Sound for the children to play on.

Future historians may have it even tougher trying to figure out the Gold Hole.

Bradshaw remembers the Gold Hole being enormous in the 1960s. "Evelyn Mayrand told me she trucked in about 25 truckloads of dirt and couldn't fill it." Dirt wasn't the only thing down there either. "I can remember when we used to put trash down there—sofas, iceboxes. Anybody who had something to get rid of, they threw it down there. I can't imagine what archaeologists are going to say 1,000 years from now."

Meanwhile, the Gold Hole continues as part of romantic lore, both on the island and off.

Phyllis A. Whitney located her 1997 mystery-romance novel, *Amethyst Dreams*, on Topsail Island. She incorporated much of the island's color—the Operation Bumblebee missile development program, the Assembly Building and tracking towers, the maritime forest, the turtle-watch program. But nothing was more central to Whitney's plot than the Gold Hole, a perfect place for a body if there ever was one. Because the real Gold Hole is on private property, Whitney explained in her preface, she moved it and renamed it the Pirate's Pit. It got a few other fictional tweaks in the process, as illustrated in this scene with narrator-heroine Hallie Knight and another key character, Anne Trench:

"WHAT IS THE PIRATE'S PIT?" I asked.

She put a dab of honey on her last bite of toast and settled back in her chair. "There are stories of hidden pirate gold all up and down the East Coast, most of them false. It wasn't gold those highwaymen of the sea hoarded—they did a fine business in all the goods they captured from sailing vessels—but the stories of gold buried on Topsail Island persisted. These stories appealed to two partners who moved onto the island to dig in a large, curious hole they'd found. They convinced others that gold was there. Investments were made in the project, and serious digging began. But in spite of digging to a great depth, nothing in the way of treasure ever surfaced. Then one night the two took the money that island people had advanced and disappeared, leaving nothing but a pit that seemed to have no bottom. Over the years people threw all sorts of things down there, including large objects that simply disappeared. The sinkhole never filled up. Anything that was dropped into it vanished."

And thus it may continue to be with the Gold Hole.

Virtually everything associated with the Gold Hole

has vanished now, including most of the hole itself and, seemingly, any chance of finding what really happened.

Only a hard-to-find hole remains, a nearly covered pit.

Only Topsail's greatest mystery.

CHAPTER FOUR

Towers

John West *passed the old missile tower numerous times long before he ever contemplated living in it.* As a child, he had come to Topsail Island on vacations from the late 1960s into the 1980s.

But Tower 4, fronting on the island's main road and with the beach at its back, now was battered and overgrown by vines. Its concrete walls had somehow been removed, leaving only the four massive corner supports and the floors. The flat roof leaked. Exposed metal reinforcements had rusted until there were literally stalactites of rust hanging from each ceiling.

Tower 4, it seemed, was no more than a worthless relic of an earlier time. Concrete. Three stories. Indestructible.

Useless.

Seven of eight observation towers remain from the post-World War II missile program, Operation Bumblebee. Most were built three stories high, but Tower 2, away from the coastline, was taller. Closest to its original condition among the structures, Tower 2 is listed on the National Register of Historic Places.

In the 1940s, the public knew nothing of Operation Bumblebee, a top-secret missile program named for the insect that, aerodynamically, should not be able to fly but does anyway.

The program was in answer to Germany's V-2 rocket assaults on France and England in 1944, according to a National Park Service history. The United States was basing its hopes on the ramjet theory advanced in 1908 by French engineer René Lorin but passed over by his government during World War II. Lorin theorized that exhaust from standard internal combustion engines, if directed into diverging nozzles, would produce jets to propel a vehicle.

After World War II, in 1945, a portion of the Camp Davis

Both Operation Bumblebee's control tower and its Assembly Building, where missiles were assembled before being launched, are included on the National Register of Historic Places. The control tower lies between the Assembly Building and the launch pad in what is now Topsail Beach. The Assembly Building now houses the Missiles and More Museum of island history, along with a community center. The launch pad is part of the patio of the Jolly Roger Motel and Pier in Topsail Beach.

area used by the Army as its Coastal Artillery Anti-Aircraft Firing Range was transferred to the Navy. By mid-1946, some 500 Navy and Marine personnel led by Lieutenant Commander Tad Stanwick arrived on the island to begin installation of the United States Naval Ordnance Test Facilities. Army soldiers from Camp Davis assisted in the building.

Operation Bumblebee arrived on the island in 1946 and would not leave until 1948. No one was allowed on the property without clearance, and even the location was secret at first. Though the Navy announced in June 1946 that it had developed a 1,500-mile-an-hour missile dubbed "the Flying Stovepipe," no mention was made of the island.

It was not until midway through the Topsail stay that official notice was given. A United States Navy press release issued March 2, 1947, said in part, "Testing of propulsion units and aerodynamic design features for missiles is scheduled to begin this month at Holly Ridge, N.C., where the facilities of Camp Davis, a former Army and Marine Corps base, have been converted to form the Naval Ordnance Test Facility." The station was being converted and operated by the Kellex Corporation, with technical guidance from the Applied Physics Laboratory of Johns Hopkins University. The missile testing would continue work that had begun on a temporary range at Fort Miles, Delaware. The release continued, "An overwater firing range parallels a sand spit adjoining the former camp site, and extends 22 miles along the coast. Eight observation stations, located along the sand spit for tracking of units in flight, will house radar and photographic equipment for recording of performance data."

The sand spit, of course, later would come to be known as Topsail Island. The observation stations would become Topsail's towers.

Operation Bumblebee tested René Lorin's idea with two-stage rockets made in Cumberland, Maryland—a solid booster to launch each small missile and a ramjet engine to boost it to supersonic speed. The missiles were put together in the Assembly Building at Topsail, taken to the ocean-side launch site a few blocks away, and fired off wood-and-iron ramps. They were sent along a northeasterly angular deflection of 15 degrees to the shoreline for a maximum clear distance of 40 miles. They were tracked from the towers.

With the help of Johns Hopkins, the Navy launched about 200 experimental rockets, ranging from three to 13 inches in diameter and formed from tailpipes of Navy Thunderbolt airplanes. The ramjet engine was an unqualified success, launching the missiles at engine speeds up to 1,400 miles an hour. The first supersonic missiles—Terrier, Talos, and Tartar—grew from the testing. Some have suggested that what occurred during Operation Bumblebee's two years also made Topsail as important to jet-propelled aircraft as Kitty Hawk was to powered flight.

In a 1970 press release for Bumblebee's 25th anniversary, the Applied Physics Laboratory at Johns Hopkins commemorated those historic events: "The APL research and development team . . . had developed a working model of the supersonic engine from only a theory in six months." In the quarter-century since the project, the press release noted, the ramjet had been tested in bigger and more powerful missiles, flying five times the speed of sound. It had been used in the Air Force's Bomarc missile and the Navy's Talos guided missile.

The Topsail days were short-lived, however. Just eight months after announcing the testing, the Navy declared the island was being abandoned. Its press release cited consolidation of facilities and funds and said that testing on the island would cease November 14, 1947. Interestingly, the Navy now said the testing facility had been operating "for the last 18 months." There also would prove to be other factors in the decision to move. As was the case with two temporary missile testing ranges that preceded it—at Island Beach, New Jersey, and Rehobeth, Delaware—Topsail had become overpopulated, or at least public boaters were coming by too often to suit the Navy. Moreover, the missiles' range was outgrowing the length of the island. And Topsail's weather was too unpredictable. So the elements of Operation Bumblebee were moved to other sites, including Inyokern in California, Cape Canaveral in Florida, and White Sands in New Mexico.

What the Navy left behind on that sand spit were structures of unsurpassed sturdiness: the Assembly Building, a nearby rocket-launching platform and bombproof shelter, a control tower, and the eight three-story observation towers spaced every couple of miles up the island. Each was built of thick, reinforced concrete. Each was virtually indestructible.

The Assembly Building went on to a variety of uses, including hardware store, nightclub, clothing store, and restaurant before sitting empty and narrowly avoiding demolition. Now, it houses the Missiles and More Museum (www.topsail missilesmuseum.org) and a community center. The building was listed on the National Register of Historic Places in 1993, along with the control tower and Tower 2, located near the Queens Grant condominiums in Topsail Beach, considered the tower closest to its original state. North Carolina historical marker D-104 stands near the control tower. It reads, "Missile Tests: U.S. Navy successfully tested ramjet engines in rocket flights, 1946-48. Observation towers line Topsail Island; Assembly Building 2 blocks west."

The launching platform is part of a patio in front of the Jolly Roger Pier and Motel. Pier developer Lewis Orr, in a 2001 recorded interview, said many people wrongly think his motel, actually a converted skating rink, was built by the Army. It was not, but the patio was, in a manner of speaking. "That concrete pad is still there, and people can see it. No pass required." He laughed. "You just walk out there and look at it or walk across it, and you're welcome." The Jolly Roger property also includes the underground bombproof shelter, complete with concrete walls and slit window. "I liken it to a bunch of kids lighting a firecracker and scrambling down to that room to watch it take off," Orr said.

And of course, the towers remain. A number have been converted into private residences. Others are vacant, battered by six decades of storms and vandals, yet still standing.

It was John West's lifelong dream to live on the ocean. He worked in the pharmaceutical industry in Raleigh, North Carolina.

Later, when he began a consulting business in 2003, West realized he could move permanently. But now, in the late 1990s, he was looking for a beach home for weekends and vacations. He considered a number of beach towns before settling on his childhood vacation island, assuming he could find the right home. West recalls knowing what wasn't the right home. The old, battered missile tower in Surf City wasn't. "My realtor, who is still a good friend, said, 'That old tower's for sale.' I said, 'No way, Patsy.' " It would be much too much work.

But the idea began to take hold. Maybe it wasn't crazy, West began to think. "The more and more I looked . . ." The tower was cheaper than most oceanfront property, for one thing. And on an island where hurricanes knock down homes, there was something to be said for an old military tower. "It has been here since 1947," West says. "It is very, very durable. I said, 'If anything withstands a hurricane, this will be it.' It had withstood the gold standard of hurricanes around here, Hurricane Hazel in '54." The tower was even 15 feet above sea level—a luxury on a barrier island—so it would be more likely than most properties to remain above the overwash from storms.

West did more research. He got the blueprints. Tower 4, as it was called in Operation Bumblebee, had been built on a 12-inch-thick slab of concrete supported by 50 to 52 pilings. Each piling was sunk 25 feet into the ground. Twenty-five feet. The result was an extraordinarily stable building, even in an unstable beach environment. "In theory, this house could be undermined by erosion and still stand," West says.

It was no mere theory. Tower 3, two miles away on the Surf City-Topsail Beach line, took a beating from Hurricane Fran in 1996. The storm ripped away a house attached to the tower and blasted away much of the sand beneath the tower,

Concrete missile towers might not seem conducive to modern living. But about half have been converted into homes, including John West's renovation of Tower Four. The showplace on Shore Drive in Surf City includes a glass-enclosed sunroom with spectacular 180-degree views of the beach and surf.

exposing some 10 feet of piling depth. Yet Tower 3, known as "Spyglass," still stands on the beach. Battered and vacant, it appears as solid as ever.

So Tower 4 would be solid, too. But even if West could clean it up, could it become a home? "The towers obviously were not designed as living quarters," he says. There were challenges nearly every square foot.

The military had built only a slim stairway against the front wall of each tower, hardly sufficient for a residence. West decided on adding a spiral staircase in the corner. That necessitated opening holes in the concrete floors, no easy chore even for experienced construction workers. "At the end of the days, these guys were tired," he says. "They were using all sorts of jackhammers and sledgehammers. All they could do was chip away a little at a time." But in the end, there was room for the staircase.

Utility lines were another problem. West couldn't burrow into concrete reinforced with steel and granite. Fortunately, each floor had a square hole and a smaller rectangular hole in the concrete. The square ones, West believes, were for dumbwaiters used to move missile-monitoring equipment from floor to floor. The smaller ones? No one knows. But the holes allowed him to slip in wiring. So did a vent apparently cut into the ceiling when a hot-dog stand had occupied the bottom floor years earlier. (The stand's existence was confirmed by a greasy black residue on the ceiling that would not take paint.) Finally, the missing walls allowed him to extend 18-inch vestibules on each side and to slip in more electrical wiring. Even the question of where to put a washer and dryer was problematic. West answered it with a space-saving stackable unit. To squeeze in a bathroom with one of the bedrooms, he put in a Jacuzzi tub instead of a full-sized bathtub. A pedestal sink saved still more room.

Still, the rooms were tiny—just 17½ feet square. Fine for military rocket observations. Not so fine for humans who don't like the life of laboratory rats. Fortunately, the missing wall on the east allowed West to build outward toward the ocean in 2002, extending each floor to nearly 30 feet. Still not spacious, but inviting. That brought an added benefit, especially on the second-floor, where a glass-enclosed sunroom offers spectacular 180-degree views of the beach and surf.

As well designed as it now is, Number 4 still is a tower. "This is not a house for people adverse to stairs," West says, laughing. "It is vertical living." On the other hand, he says, finding the silver lining, it offers terrific exercise. The exercise was enhanced when West changed the flat roof to a pitched one, giving him a "cupola," meaning a fourth floor with a small bedroom. Access, though, comes by climbing a captain's ladder to what apparently was a hatch hole in the roof. Putting in traditional stairs was not possible.

In the winter of 2005-6, West made more changes. By now, he was living on the island full time. His tower wasn't quite a home, though. "That's not how the place was designed. It was a weekend getaway." He converted the bottom floor into a bedroom and den. The middle floor became the main living area, complete with a sunroom, kitchen, and dining room. The entrance from the street now comes in at this level, too. The third floor is another bedroom. Splitting the main bedrooms gives privacy to each, West says. Otherwise, a guest would have to walk through one to get to the other.

The tower also has something money can't buy: two four-inch brass United States Coast and Geodetic Survey markers. The Coast and Geodetic Survey, whose work has now been taken over by the National Geodetic Survey, was a successor to an agency started under President Thomas Jefferson to reduce the number of shipwrecks by surveying the country's coastline. Each of the official markers is engraved with "Tower Four 1947." One is in what is now a downstairs storage room. The other is embedded in the cupola's floor on what used to be the roof.

West's tower, an eyesore when he came upon it, is now one of the island's eye-catchers. "Had I known all this stuff, I probably would not have done it," he admits. He figures he'll never stop working on it. "I guess ignorance truly is bliss. But now that I'm this far along, I wouldn't take anything for it." He could name his price. "These things are in high demand. I get calls from people all the time: 'Are you interested in selling?' "

So why isn't he? "It's a great place to live," West says. "I love the area. I love the people. The people are more laid-back. . . . You can start up a conversation with a cashier at the grocery store easier than in the city. There are no nightclubs, only one fast-food place. People ask, 'Where are the attractions?' To me, those are the attractions. It's almost like a step back in time."

In this case, all the way back to the 1940s.

Through the years, Operation Bumblebee, though no longer top secret, has remained mysterious. Even as late as the summer of 1987, Claude Moore, writing the "Our Heritage" column in the *Pender Chronicle*, said, "I have been going to Topsail Island for more than 35 years and only recently did I learn about [it]."

There was no dearth of newspaper and magazine articles in the 1980s and even earlier about the missile program. There was simply a dearth of information.

In a lengthy *Fayetteville Observer* article on September 24, 1978, Dick Brown reported that no evidence existed in the National Archives or military records: "Despite its importance in any timetable of missile development, details of the operation 'Bumblebee' are shrouded in red tape and mystery and buried deeply somewhere in dusty, neglected military records."

That surprised the Applied Physics Laboratory spokesman who only eight years earlier had written the 25th-anniversary press release bragging about the program. "This was a major program, the forerunner of the Talos and all other Navy guided missiles," spokesman C. J. O'Brien said.

There was physical evidence, of course. "Tracking towers, looking like squared-off silos and numbering eight in all, that once dotted the barren shoreline have been converted into homes and offices," Brown wrote. "And one provided sanctuary for the only islander who chose to ride out Hurricane

Hazel." Through records at the Applied Physics Laboratory at Johns Hopkins, Brown pieced together the Bumblebee story. Particularly helpful was Irvine B. Irving, then still a member of the Johns Hopkins lab staff. Irvine was quoted as saying lab personnel visited the island in 1945, moved onto it in March 1946, and were launching test missiles by October or November. Nearly 200 were fired before the program departed the island in early 1948.

Still, misinformation and mythology grew around the top-secret program. Brown noted in 1978 that a chamber-of-commerce brochure mistakenly called the experimental work a forerunner of the Cape Canaveral space program. Joseph Baneth Allen wrote frequently on Topsail's towers for magazines and journals in the 1980s—in *The State* in July 1985, in *Encore* in 1986, and in the *Journal of the Council on America's Past* in the summer of 1991, for instance—noting other common myths. For one, the towers were mistakenly thought to have been built for observing German submarine activity during World War II. For another, the towers were mistakenly thought to be forerunners of buildings at Cape Canaveral.

But Brown and Allen themselves wrote that the Operation Bumblebee missiles were transferred from the Assembly Building to the launch pad via an underground tunnel, an idea that itself has since been largely discredited. Allen cited a claim by a crew laying sewer pipe in 1978 that it had come across a tunnel. Likewise, Brown wrote, "An underground tunnel, built to connect the assembly building on the sound-side with the launch area, was long ago covered with blacktop streets, and accidentally rediscovered recently by a crew laying a new sewer line." Brown quoted no less an authority than Irvine, who had been at the scene. "Missiles were assembled in a building over on the sound side," Irvine said, "and moved

North Carolina historical marker D-104, temporarily down
for pole repairs in this picture, tells the story: "Missile Tests: U.S.
Navy successfully tested ramjet engines in rocket flights, 1946-48.
Observation towers line Topsail Island;
Assembly Building 2 blocks west."

on dollies through an underground tunnel or topside by truck
to the launch area."

The existence of a tunnel was a widely held belief, and
even a romantic one. It could be comical as well. A videotape
now at the museum shows longtime island residents considering the question, edited to make it appear they are debating
it. Back and forth it goes: some believe in the tunnel, some do
not. David A. Stallman, in his 1996 *Echoes of Topsail*, seemed
to get a more definitive answer, quoting Jim Heathcoat, whose
technical-support duties at the time of Operation Bumblebee
had included maintaining tower cameras. Heathcoat said he
often was asked about the tunnel. He knew firsthand the real
story: "The 'secret tunnel' was a steel conduit about 10 inches

in diameter that ran from the control tower to the launch ramp. This conduit was crammed full of control cables."

But there is nothing secret about Topsail's towers, which stand with one exception as the island's most visible reminders of the military's presence. The northernmost one, Tower 8, on the oceanfront in what is now North Topsail Beach, became a popular spot for late-night parties and vandalism in the decades after the program. Three people, in separate incidents, fell to their deaths from the third story. Two of the deaths came in August 1986: Michelle Hobbs, a 28-year-old, who fell early in the month; and Marine sergeant Daniel S. Campbell, who fell during an early-morning party late in the month. Tower 8 was torn down a few years later.

The rest of Topsail's unique towers remain, coastal sentinels likely to withstand the ravages of the island for generations to come.

~~~~~~~

CHAPTER FIVE

Piers

*I*t *is 6:40 on an October morning.* Sunrise is approaching. The waves crash on the beach, louder, it seems, than during daylight hours. The air is cooler, damper, the breeze seemingly stiffer. Later in the day, shirts and shorts will be fine. But for now, this is jacket weather.

The only light comes from the Surf City Pier, stretching out over the Atlantic. Lights atop poles send small, dim glows into the mist. The lighting is enough only to suggest shapes. There seem to be people on the pier already.

A red-yellow glow appears across the horizon, muted at first, then more commanding. It is a scene of serenity: waves rolling onto the beach, a pier extending into the mist, the awakening sun illuminating it with more artistry than a lighting-effects expert ever could.

The first rays of the day also bring the shapes out of hiding. Dozens of people, perhaps scores, are on the pier. Their faces are still unclear. But their fishing poles extend upward against the railing. A thin line drops from each into the surf. Some have been here for hours already. Some will be here all day.

There are few better places to be than a fishing pier.

Commercial and individual fishermen mined the waters of Topsail from boats or the beach except when the military controlled the island in the 1930s and 1940s. Fishing resumed after the military left in 1948 and was made easier by the pontoon bridge it left behind. Most of the early postwar fishermen were content to stand on the beach and cast their lines into the surf or to drop them from boats into the sound or the ocean.

But they were happier when the piers showed up.

There have been as many as nine piers on Topsail at one time—eight on the ocean and one on Topsail Sound. Piers come and go on Topsail, battered by storms, rebuilt, given new names, let go. Even the start-up dates have been debated. An article in the June 1967 issue of *The State* magazine said Topsail had the largest concentration of fishing piers on the North Carolina coast, including the Surf City Pier (built in 1952; actually in 1953), New Topsail Ocean Pier (1953; actually 1954), Barnacle Bill's Pier (1956), Paradise Pier (1958), Dolphin Pier (1960), McKee's New River Inlet Pier (1960), and Scotch Bonnet Pier (1967). The black-owned Ocean City Pier, not mentioned, opened in 1959.

Storms and economics have claimed most of them. Now, only one remains in each island town: the Seaview Pier in North Topsail Beach, the Surf City Pier in Surf City, and the Jolly Roger Pier in Topsail Beach. Each has had an important history and faces an uncertain future.

Lewis Orr built what would become the Jolly Roger Pier in 1954, then immediately lost it to Hurricane Hazel. He rebuilt, which he would do again and again through the years, all the while adding a restaurant and a motel—right at the spot America had launched some of its first missiles. Lewis Orr died in 2005. But four years earlier, Topsail Beach's first mayor told his story as only he could. Evelyn Bradshaw, one of the island's de facto historians, sat down with Orr to record the experience. She had to do little more than turn on the tape recorder.

Listen:

"I guess this story starts for me in the pier business in 1954, when we built our pier. We were the second one on the island. Surf City was first, and we came back the next year. We didn't want to let those boys get all the money.

"In those days, it was a different economy than we have now. We're talking 1954. At that time, eastern Carolina was built around tobacco farms. And it was just very fortunate that the end of the tobacco season coincided with the big run of fall fish here at Topsail Beach. So the farmers were taking their money in and looking for a place to put it, as we all do when we get some money. They found they could come to the beach and fish. It was a good investment in some sense because they'd take home oodles of fish and go home and have Sunday dinners, fish fries. It was just an institution to come to the beach in the fall and fish."

The pier opened April 1. A big storm—it would have been called a hurricane had it hit in the fall—took away 200 feet of the pier. Almost immediately, then, Orr was rebuilding.

"Things were going along fine until October 15, 1954," he continued. "A lady named Hazel paid us a visit, and she took down the whole pier. There was no way we could rebuild and reopen for the remainder of the season." Orr began to rebuild for 1955. "First of all, we picked up all the lumber that was washed up on the beach. The long pilings that were out on the end of the pier had broken about the sand line—the top of whatever the depth of the water was, down to the sand line. They were in the ground about 15 feet. So take 15 feet off a 60-foot piling and you still have a piling you can use on the way out to the end in shallow water. So we got a few of those we could use. A lot of the lumber we picked up, and backed the nails out of it, the spikes out of it, and started rebuilding."

The pier initially was called the New Topsail Ocean Fishing Pier, a name chosen to reflect its location on the island's ocean side near New Topsail Inlet. But the name proved awkward for advertising and news stories. The area had been known as New Topsail through J. G. Anderson's early real-estate development, but when local leaders, Orr among them, incorporated the area into a town in 1963, they decided it, too, was due for a name change. They chose Topsail Beach. That coincided with Orr's business expansion—he bought the Anderson-built skating rink immediately north of the pier and converted it into a motel—and with the renaming of his pier. "We wanted a name that would be euphonic—have a good ring to it—and we wanted a name that was historical and nautical and was catchy, people would remember it," Orr said. "So we came up with this idea of the Jolly Roger Pier and then incorporated the motel in that name, so that when we advertise, we could kill two cats with one stone."

Fishing was still the island's primary lure, not vacationers. "The fishing in the early days, the most popular fish was the spot, especially with farmers and local people. In the early days, local people was about it. We didn't have many 'snowbirds' down here and people from all over eastern North Carolina. . . . The spot would come in by the millions, and anybody could catch 'em. It didn't require any special skill. You bought a little shrimp and put it on a hook and drop it to the bottom, and you'd better be fast because he was on it in a minute."

There were no coolers in those days. The farmers who came down to fish put their catches in six-gallon metal cans, which sold for a dollar. "Incidentally, tickets then started off at 75 cents." Pier operators have continually had to raise the price of those fishing tickets since then. Orr laughed. "Some people wondered if that's the way we got the name Jolly Roger—we named it after the pirates, and the pirates are still around."

While the farmers fished for spot and Virginia mullet, or whiting, the sportfishermen were going after bluefish and Spanish mackerel. "This was about the time that spinning reels came in, and they just fitted them perfectly with that type of fishing. Spot fishing ran through the fall, along with the others. We had a lot of flounders, puppy drum, bluefish, Spanish mackerel—you name it, we had it." The big fish were caught at the end of the pier. More were coming. "Around that time, the first tarpon in North Carolina was caught . . . south of here, maybe Wrightsville Beach. So that started us thinking." Orr himself had hooked a tarpon in Panama, though he hadn't been able to reel it in. "But I'll never forget it because they are strong, powerful, beauty—everything you could want in a sports fish."

Orr began promoting tarpon fishing at the Jolly Roger Pier. "Dr. Earl Rubwright of Jacksonville landed a monster out there. Well, that made all the newspapers—first pier in North Carolina history to catch a tarpon. We were mighty proud of that, and needless to say, we didn't try to hold the news back. We spread it all up and down the state. So tarpon became a big thing. I don't mean they caught a lot, but they tried a lot."

Reeling in a big fish often takes two men, including one with a stick that has a large hook at the end. Orr said:

THE TRICK ON THIS BIG FISHING IS YOU HANG A BIG FISH AND LET YOUR DRAG OFF AND LET THE FISH RUN AND TRY TO GET HIM AWAY FROM THE PIER, AND THEN YOU WEAR HIM DOWN AND BRING HIM IN. And then we drop a gaff down, somebody else does, and a gaff man brings him up. If you bring him in too green, he'll go underneath that pier and cut the line on those barnacles. They do that on the king mackerel.

On the tarpon, it's much the same except they let the fish run and they get him as far from the pier as they can. Then the fisherman runs the length of the pier with the rod. He has a buddy who goes down on the beach. The fisherman hands the rod to his buddy, and his buddy takes off running away from the pier as fast as he can, with the fisherman trying to catch up to him. The point of all that is you want to get that tarpon away from the pier so he won't go underneath the pier and cut his line. That's one of the sickest feelings for a fisherman, to have a beautiful fish, fight him for an hour or two, and then have him go under the pier and cut the line.

That's quite a show, and it draws a crowd. And it'll be an hour or two before that man draws him in, and all the people from the cottages come pouring out to watch the show. So that's part of the fun we have.

Storms meant periodically rebuilding all or part of the pier. "In those days, you could get insurance from Lloyd's of London, and they enabled us to rebuild," Orr said. "Now, it's just too expensive to do anything, and you're damned if you do and damned if you don't on that insurance business. Some of the piers have it and some don't. . . . We used to have eight piers down here. . . . One of them burned down, a couple others were lost to storms, just went out of business. Ended up, we just had Surf City Pier and mine, just like it started. Several others have come in over the years."

But Orr wouldn't have given it up for the world.

"It was nice working there. It never was a job to me. I enjoyed the people. I've often said I don't see how you could be a doctor. I don't see how a doctor could stand it. Everyone comes in there griping, feeling bad. Down here, people come in feeling good."

Orr's son Robin is the pier's manager now. Robin, his brother Lewis Jr., and their sister Teresa bought the Jolly Roger from their father well before he died. The business is more challenging these days, Robin says. Everything from hurricanes to the increasing cost of gasoline to competing forms of recreation has an effect on the number of people fishing. The family has no plans to sell the pier, though. "It's what we do," Robin says. "It's as much a way of life as a job."

One of the pier's best fisherman was Angelo De Paola, nicknamed "Deep," Orr said. "He has fished more hours on that pier than any human being and has caught more kingfish." De Paola even caught a large sailfish, normally something found in deep water.

De Paola is still fishing on Topsail Island, as he has for well over a half-century. Sitting in the restaurant of the Jolly Roger Pier, Deep doesn't dispute Orr's claims. But he modestly places them in perspective: "I just put in a lot of hours." He tries to fish nearly every day, beginning in early April.

Nearly all his fishing is from the pier. He began fishing in the surf in 1951 or 1952, then switched to Orr's pier in 1955. The pier opened in 1954, but De Paola couldn't get down to the island for a few weeks. When he did, he found Hazel had destroyed the pier.

De Paola was born in Italy in 1920, came to New Jersey in 1929, and grew up a child of the Depression. In 1940, he enlisted in the Marines. He met his future wife, Janet, while she was living in New Bern, North Carolina, and he was stationed at Camp Lejeune near Jacksonville. There, he met his second love, Topsail. After World War II, De Paola returned to a career in the Camp Lejeune Fire Department, retiring in 1975. Through the years, except when he was overseas with the Marines, he fished at Topsail. In 1979, he and Janet moved to the island.

In the early days, De Paola fished for sea mullet in the spring, bluefish in the late spring, and Spanish mackerel after that. Then came 1957. "Somebody noticed in May and June that some shiny fish were jumping out there," De Paola says. Dallas Ritter, a charter-boat operator on the weekends and fisherman during the week, knew they were king mackerel. Big fish. That summer, three tarpon and four king mackerel were caught, De Paola says. "Lewis Orr said, 'I'm going to give $100 to anybody who catches a tarpon.' Well, it cost him $300."

De Paola made the switch the following year. "In 1958, I decided I was going to quit this small stuff and fish big game— king mackerel and tarpon." The average tarpon weighs 70 to 80 pounds. De Paola remembers at least six 100-pounders that have been pulled from the Topsail Beach waters over the years. Just over 50 of all sizes have been caught by Jolly Roger fishermen, an average of only one a year. "I've landed six of those things, from 62 to 110 pounds." He adds with a smile, "Some lady fishing out here caught one that weighed 112 pounds." De Paola also has caught 490 king mackerel—yes, he keeps detailed records—all but three or four at the Jolly Roger. He's caught about 25 large cobia.

De Paola remembers when Topsail fishing was even better. Big drum used to be plentiful; he's seen two or three in the last 30 years. Likewise amberjacks; he hasn't seen any in a decade. "Forty years ago, I could come out on this pier and catch fish all day long during a spot run." Commercial fishing has taken a lot of the catch now. Island development, which affects fish like the drum, has increased. Then, too, De Paola blames old-time fishermen like himself for not throwing back the big fish they caught. "We didn't know any better. We caught hundreds of them, thousands of them, and none of them were released." De Paola now is a member of the Coastal Conservation Association. "We're trying to curtail some of this."

Farther north, in Surf City, stands the island's first pier, or at least its latest incarnation.

The Surf City Pier was opened in 1953 by Hugh Barwick, Sr., of Clinton, North Carolina. The opening came later than the intended October 15 completion date. Hurricane Florence, though not making a direct hit on the island, had stirred the sea enough to break up the pier just a few weeks earlier. The pier, planned to be 1,000 feet long, was three-quarters complete. An unusually high wave took off two 12-foot sections at the end, along with a pile driver, according to the *Pender Chronicle*. Reporter Irene Clark wrote, "A spectator who viewed the collapse of the pier stated that he 'saw it coming. . . . I just had begun to think that the high tide (which was at 11:06 that morning) wasn't going to hurt the pier, although the constant crashing of the waves at the end had weakened it, when out at sea I saw that last great big wave forming. "If she breaks at the end of the pier, that'll do it," I said to myself. And sure enough, it did.' "

Ed Lore owns the pier now. His father, the late Ed Lore, Jr., bought it in 1973, when he was 45. "My dad loved to trout-fish," says his son, who was 11 then. "He wanted to be down here near the trout." His mother, Lore says, never would move from their home in Smithfield, North Carolina.

The son mostly fished. There wasn't much else to do. "In the '70s, I called it 'the ghost town,' " Lore says with a laugh. "I used to call it 'the last frontier.' There were just a couple restaurants and gift shops. No Hardee's, no Domino's, no Pizza Hut . . . Now, it's been discovered. It's grown more in the last five years than in the previous 30."

It's not always easy making a go of it, though. Piers, Lore says, are an endangered species. Storms. Economics. Insurance.

In 1954, "Hazel got all but the tackle shop," he says. That meant both the island's new piers were gone. A 1963 storm damaged the Surf City Pier, too, Lore believes. In 1973, the pier was rebuilt with steel pilings, which would prove a bad idea because of rusting. One year later, in 1974, the pier went down. "It was just a nor'easter," he says.

Insurance costs escalated to the point that Lore dropped coverage on the pier in 1985, just before Hurricane Gloria hit. "I threw $30,000 in the water," he says. The year 1996 was doubly difficult. "Bertha took the end and the piece between the dune and the base. Fran took it all out." Islanders learn to live with hurricanes, as inexplicable as that may sound to mainlanders. That's particularly true of fishing-pier operators. "I would be comfortable with a Category 2, even a direct hit," Lore says. Bertha was a 2, Fran a 3. "A Category 3, I don't know. A Category 4, forget it."

The Surf City Pier has one of Topsail's prime locations. For those crossing the swing bridge onto the island, it is directly ahead on the beach. The wooden pier is 900 feet long now—actually 937 to the door of the shop. Lore has had sev-

The Surf City Pier attracts hundreds with their fishing rods on a sunny October day. Opened in 1953, the pier has had to be at least partly rebuilt many times after storms, as have the others on the island. Topsail once had nine piers. Now only Surf City, the Jolly Roger, and the Seaview remain.

eral offers to buy it. Like the Orrs in Topsail Beach, he says at least for now, he's not selling.

Lore virtually lives at the pier in October. To a pier operator, October is what December is to a retailer—the month you make your money. "Spots are money fish." Schools of them swim by in October. On an October day, 300 to 400 people will show up, sometimes 600, Lore says. They come from North Carolina, of course, but a good many arrive from as far away as Ohio and Pennsylvania. Many stay a week.

Like the other two piers, Surf City's is open to those who want to walk it for just one dollar. The Surf City Pier offers another value for island aficionados. In 2004, Lore let East

A glowing sunrise silhouettes the Surf City Pier on a November morning. A few pier walkers are already up.

Coast Sports put up an Internet camera on his pier. Now, those who want to keep Topsail near can have the surf on their computers at www.eastcoastsports.com and www.renta beach.com/webcam/. The image of waves, beach, and pier are continually updated.

On an October weekend, the Surf City Pier is packed.

Men and boys, along with more women and girls than fished in the early days, are planted every few feet. Their rods angle up to the sky, their lines dropping into the water. They carry on conversations with neighbors, abbreviated in the way old friends carry on conversations.

Most on the pier are fishing, but a few people are there just to walk or take a few pictures. The breeze is up but warm. The surf crashes far below.

There are not many better places to be than a fishing pier.

Farther north, in North Topsail Beach, is the remaining pier, Seaview.

Greg Ludlum has owned it since 2000. "As best they can tell, it was built in 1984," he says. "There are no records. There's not even a record for this building."

The pier building—now housing an office and a small restaurant—is an unusual one. The small vertical structure was angled to avoid direct hits from storms, and it has stood when other buildings have toppled. It never even loses shingles or siding, Ludlum says. Even odder, the dark brown building has music symbols on its side. "It was a music studio, poker house, whorehouse," Ludlum says matter-of-factly. Those were the days when this part of the island was West Onslow Beach, where regulations were few. A number of musicians recorded

Greg Ludlum, owner of the Seaview Pier

One of the island's more unusual structures is the Seaview Pier building in North Topsail Beach. Angled to deflect high winds, the brown building has withstood storms and even hurricanes. The guitar and piano on the side reflect its days as a music studio where the likes of Boxcar Willie recorded.

here, including Boxcar Willie, he says. Many flew into a small private airport that was within walking distance.

It was known as Salty's Pier when it was taken down by a 1993 nor'easter, the so-called storm of the century, Ludlum says. Rebuilt in 1998-99, it was stronger, a 960-foot-long structure with more than 200 pilings. Even so, the Seaview was damaged during Hurricane Ophelia in 2005, though not by the storm itself. Debris from homes and decks and dune crossovers up the beach were the culprits. The raging surf slammed them into his pier, taking out 19 pilings at the end. Repairs were made over the 2005-6 off-season.

Tourism and developers have taken to North Topsail Beach with a passion in the 21st century. That's not necessarily good for a fishing pier. Wealthy property owners don't frequent the pier, Ludlum says, at least not in large-enough numbers. As property values have skyrocketed, few fishermen living on the island have been able to stay. "It used to be, a pier would do 100,000 people a year," Ludlum says. "We're doing 30,000." Meanwhile, taxes are $10,000 a year. Insurance is $50,000 a year—and comes with a $150,000 deductible. Rebuilding the pier in its entirety would cost at least $750,000, and probably more. "It's hand-to-mouth just to run one of these things down here."

Ludlum does two-thirds of his business in September and October, he says. The pier thrives during those months. But there's not enough business to warrant keeping it open for the four months beginning December 1.

Ludlum intends to stay—if he can. "It's not for sale, but I'm not crazy either," he says. The pier property is big enough for seven homes. If the right offer came along, he would have to sell it. "To me, it's a good living," he says. "Tore down, it's a good retirement." Ludlum has done the math, in other words. Call it the new Topsail math: "This property with the pier is worth $2.5 million," he says. "Without the pier, this is worth $4 million." Ludlum even signed a deal to sell the pier. The buyer died. In hindsight, Ludlum is glad the sale wasn't completed. "You're not talking about selling your pier, you're talking about selling your life."

Even on a December morning, with few people around, the Seaview Pier is alive. The sun shines, the gulls fly, the surf pounds. The glare off the ocean is so bright, not even sunglasses cut it completely. A visitor has to squint.

Below, a lone runner on the sand approaches the pier, goes underneath, and emerges from the other side. He keeps up a good pace but stays in sight well up the beach. The view from up here is unsurpassed. There are not many better places to be than a fishing pier.

Those fortunate enough to have walked one of Topsail's piers, or fished or taken pictures from it, can only hope the owners put off selling.

Time on a pier is worth more than anyone could pay for it.

CHAPTER SIX

Hurricanes

Nothing matters so much on Topsail Island as hurricanes. Residents remember them vividly, whether a decade or a half-century later. Lives are at best disrupted. At worst, they are ruined or even lost.

And yet the islanders live with hurricanes. They are a part of life, like sunsets or a run of spots—though with the potential to kill. The big winds rise in late summer and continue through the fall, and always Topsail is vulnerable. Islanders and late-summer tourists may be blissfully unaware of other news events, but they keep up with the national hurricane trackers. They tune in to the Weather Channel.

Early records are spotty. But an 1899 hurricane—unnamed, as they were in those days—was newsworthy. The *Wilmington Messenger* reported November 4, 1899, "Mr.

George Shepard, of Topsail Sound, was in the city yesterday and told a *Messenger* representative that the storm damaged him fully $300 in the destruction of boats and damage to sound front property."

Many hurricanes have hit the island through the years. Jay Barnes's definitive work, *North Carolina's Hurricane History*, has documented a number.

Hurricane Donna, for instance, came ashore near Topsail Island in September 1960. Winds gusted in excess of 100 miles an hour, and tides ran four to eight feet above normal. Donna would kill eight people in eastern North Carolina. A large flock of sea gulls was even caught in the storm's eye—an occurrence confirmed by military radar. Their bodies would wash up on Topsail and other beaches.

Hurricane Ginger struck Atlantic Beach in September 1971, bringing less-than-hurricane-strength wind gusts of 58 miles an hour to Topsail Beach.

Newspaper accounts say a strong northeaster hit Topsail in 1985, ripping out the bottom floor of the oceanfront Sea Vista Motel in Topsail Beach, which led Pender County officials to condemn it until the owners moved it farther from the sea. A 1993 nor'easter, which traveled from Cuba to Canada and was dubbed "the storm of the century," took down one of the island's fishing piers.

The slow-moving Hurricane Bonnie of August 1998 was remembered in each town, doing $1.8 million worth of damage in Topsail Beach, breaching rebuilt sand dunes and flipping at least five trailers into the sound in Surf City, and tearing down 60 percent of a new dune wall, damaging 600 homes, and doing $2.5 million worth of damage in North Topsail Beach.

Hurricane Floyd in 1999 brought sustained winds of 96 miles an hour to the island and gusts of 123. Winds and flooding leveled man-made dunes at the northern end, cut three new inlets across the island, and damaged homes and power poles.

In 2005, Hurricane Ophelia stayed offshore and pounded Topsail with high winds and flooding for three days. Homes were damaged. Protective sand dunes, wooden walkovers, and the beach itself were wiped away in many areas. Again, the north end was hit hardest. Eight duplexes were condemned and ordered torn down by the town of North Topsail Beach because the high-tide line had moved behind them.

For residents of Topsail, two storm years stand out above all others: 1954 and 1996.

Nineteen-fifty-four for Hurricane Hazel.

Nineteen-ninety-six for Hurricane Fran, right on the heels of Hurricane Bertha.

Hurricane Hazel, the first "storm of the century" for Topsail, caught many by surprise. The United States Weather Bureau had issued "northeast storm warnings" from Charleston, South Carolina, to Virginia the day before Hazel came ashore. Newspapers ran stories about the devastation Hazel had visited upon the island nation of Haiti. But North Carolinians on the whole were not panicked, if they were even aware. Hurricanes had bypassed the state for years. Media coverage lacked the immediacy and urgency of today's hurricane warnings. There was no Weather Channel or 24-hour cable news or satellite view for local forecasters. Moreover, forecasters believed the storm was headed for the Outer Banks.

The next day, October 15, 1954, Hazel came ashore near the South Carolina line and headed north. It carried sustained winds of 140 miles an hour—a virtually unheard-of Category 4 hurricane. As devastating as the wind speed was the timing of the landfall. Hazel came ashore at high tide, and, worse still, it was the highest lunar tide of the year. The catastrophic coupling resulted in a storm surge of more than 17 feet in some places. Overwash at Topsail and points south was unlike anything residents had ever seen or even heard about.

Fortunately, there were few tourists. Beach towns in the 1950s essentially emptied out after Labor Day weekend. Even so, 19 people were killed along North Carolina's coast. The property damage was substantial—about $136 million worth in North Carolina, the equivalent of $930 million in dollars measured a half-century later. President Eisenhower declared the Carolina coast a disaster area.

Topsail Island had been opened only a half-dozen years for residential development. There were few homes on the Onslow County portion of the island, which now includes North Topsail Beach. But in Pender County, which included the new communities of Surf City and what would become Topsail Beach, damage was cataclysmic. The bridge was carried away at Surf City, and a Marine Corps amphibious vehicle was the only means of transport to the island for days. At New Topsail Beach—later to become the town of Topsail Beach—210 of the 230 houses were destroyed and property damage was estimated at $2.5 million. The newly built New Topsail Ocean Pier, which would become the Jolly Roger Pier, was also taken down.

Even buildings that survived the storm were not safe. Overwash from the Atlantic Ocean flooded the island. Many homes that were not destroyed were simply lifted off their foundations and swept into the sound or the marshes behind the island.

Barry Newsome, one of Topsail Beach's leading civic volunteers and either a visitor or resident on the island since 1952, remembers his family losing its home. Literally. "We found part of our house in the sound," he says. Much of it was oddly intact, like the kitchen cabinets. "The cups were still on the hangers." Hurricane Fran in 1996 would leave debris everywhere, Newsome says. But in 1954, Hazel, hitting a little-occupied island, simply leveled it. "You could see ocean and sound at the same time."

Bill Cherry, who now owns the Breezeway Motel and Restaurant with his wife, Kathy, has survived many of the island's hurricanes. Few stories top his encounter with Hazel. "I was the last one off the island, they tell me," says Cherry, a boy at the time. The family departed over the military pontoon bridge at Surf City. "When we got on it, the pontoons just popped. The bridge swung up and hit the back of the car. I was in the backseat." Fortunately, no one was hurt. But no one else was leaving on that bridge either.

Dewey and Eunice Justice, who ran what was then called the Breez-way Inn and Café, returned after Hazel to find 34 inches of water in the dining room, according to a March 1985 article in *Cape Fear Tidewater* magazine. Only 10 of the 300 homes on the island were still standing.

Hazel scared off would-be builders for several years. Doug Medlin, whose father was one of the island's early entrepreneurs, says Surf City had been growing quickly from a fishing outpost. "When Hazel came through in '54, it knocked it back for a while." Most of the homes had been "bare-bones cottages" built right on the ground. "Entire houses went into the sound."

Hurricane Hazel did have one positive effect. Before the storm, cottages had been constructed on concrete slabs, making it easy for them to slide off during flooding. After the hurricane, new homes were elevated on pilings.

It would be a year or more until the island began to resemble something other than a war zone, though.

Before: North Topsail Beach oceanfront homes in July 1996.
Hurricane Bertha, a category 2 storm, has just hit,
leaving behind beach and dune erosion.
(U.S. Geological Service's Center for Coastal Geology)

Fortunately, it would be more than four decades before the island faced a comparable storm.

Topsail's second "storm of the century" was Hurricane Fran, a Category 3 storm that hit the island in September 1996. Fran's effect was intensified by coming just two months after Hurricane Bertha, a Category 2. Topsail was the island hit hardest by Bertha. Then Topsail was the island hit hardest by Fran.

The combination would cripple the island.

Bertha arrived on July 12 and 13, 1996, North Carolina's first July hurricane since 1908. It hit the coast just below Topsail with winds of over 100 miles an hour. Boasting a 35-mile-wide eye, Bertha washed away dunes and battered homes with its strong offshore winds. Topsail took the highest sustained storm surge—estimated between five and eight feet—of any island. All of its three towns suffered extensive structural damage and flooding. There was an unconfirmed report of a 144-mile-an-hour gust at Topsail Beach.

Barnes wrote:

NORTH TOPSAIL BEACH, VIEWED BY SOME AS HAVING TOO LITTLE ELEVATION FOR RESIDENTIAL DEVELOPMENT, WAS HARDEST HIT BY THE OCEAN SURGE. Waves rolled over the area's modest dunes and flooded State Route 1568, washing away tons of sand and causing the road to collapse in at least three sections. As the storm passed, pools of water up to ten feet deep crossed the broken highway that provided the only access to the northern tip of the island. More than two miles of the road's northernmost ends were buried in sand. According to the *Raleigh News and Observer*, about fifteen families were stranded in their cottages beyond the scuttled road, and emergency personnel considered sending a Marine Corps helicopter to rescue them. . . .

As Bertha bore down on Topsail Island, police in Surf City rescued more than fifty people who had belatedly decided not to weather the storm. According to a report in *The Savage Season*, published by the *Wilmington Star-News*, Police Chief David Jones endured another of the storm's close calls. "We went to get a lady that was up at the north end, and we got out of the car trying to get to her house, and the roof picked up off her house and just missed the patrol car and us by about six feet," Jones reported. "A whole roof crashed in the road in front of us."

North Topsail lost more than just sand dunes and State Road (S.R.) 1568. More than 120 homes were destroyed, and hundreds more suffered damage from wind and water. Some structures remained visibly intact, even though their ground-floor garages and utility rooms were swept clean by the rush of water. Dozens of washers, dryers, heat pumps and other appliances were washed into ditches and marshes, forming instant landfills. Scattered among the broken and exposed water mains were cars, buried to their door handles in deep sand. The walls of some homes were peeled open, their contents visible to the outside like oversized doll houses. These were the scenes that attracted television news crews in the days and weeks following Bertha, as North Topsail Beach was generally considered to have borne the brunt of the storm's fury.

The rest of the island fared badly as well, and it didn't help that the early storm arrived during the height of the tourist season. Fishing piers were heavily damaged. Homes and shops were damaged. The beach was severely eroded. Worse for some island residents, officials would not allow them back to see their homes until the area was deemed safe enough. Topsail Beach officials, for instance, did not open the area until July 15, and even then residents were only allowed to tour the town on school buses.

When they finally were allowed back on Topsail to stay, the islanders set to cleaning up as quickly as they could.

The same homes in September 1996, following Hurricane Fran, a category 3 storm. Damage far beyond erosion is visible now. Homes have been destroyed, overwash has gouged out the beach in numerous places, and the island's main road has been breached.
(U.S. Geological Service's Center for Coastal Geology)

Little did they know.
The worst was yet to come.

Hurricane Fran, another "storm of the century" for Topsail, came ashore September 5 and 6, 1996, with maximum sustained winds of 115 miles an hour, enough to qualify as a Category 3 storm.

The National Oceanographic and Atmospheric Administration's hurricane research division later would discover why Fran brought such damage and flooding to Topsail in particular. The researchers charted Fran's sustained hurricane-category winds—those of 74 miles an hour or greater—and found that the area just off Topsail had exposure of eight straight hours. The island itself was exposed for seven straight hours, the longest time any land area was battered by Fran. Few structures could stand up to the force. The foundations of oceanfront houses were pounded so long the homes simply gave up and went into the sea.

After being softened up by Bertha, little Topsail Island had no defenses left for the fury of Fran. Barnes wrote,

BERTHA [HAD] CAUSED EXTENSIVE PROPERTY DAMAGES, BUT MORE IMPORTANT, IT WASHED AWAY THE ISLAND'S PROTECTIVE DUNES. Afterward, very little remained to slow the ten-foot storm surge that accompanied Fran. . . .

The devastation at Topsail was immense. Nearly all of the front-row cottages in Topsail Beach were destroyed, and about half of the second-row homes were either destroyed or heavily damaged. Flights over the island on the morning after the storm were the only means of assessing the scope of the loss. Along one three-mile stretch of N.C. 50 in Surf City, the *News and Observer* estimated, about 200 out of the 500 homes had "obvious roofs and walls missing, foundations crumbled, or windows blown in." In many locations, splintered stubs of pilings and half-exposed septic tanks were the only recognizable features that remained where houses had once stood. More than 300 homes incurred damages that exceeded half their value. Added to the debris on the beach were hundreds of car tires torn loose from an artificial reef about five miles offshore.

North Topsail was also hit hard again. It was estimated that more than 90 percent of the structures in town were either destroyed or damaged beyond repair. Many had never been fully restored after Bertha, but others had been completely re-modeled. Some unfortunate homeowners had just finished repairs during the week of Fran's arrival. After Fran, the town hall and police station were gone, and roadways and utilities that had been patched together after Bertha were demolished. The tide that swept over the island was so power-ful that it lifted entire cottages and floated them hundreds of yards into the marsh. Its force was so strong, in fact, that it carved six new inlets across Topsail Island, slicing up the beach road and iso-lating entire communities.

Amazingly, scores of residents remained in their island homes as Fran came ashore, though not all of them wanted to be there. Several said they simply waited too late to leave and found themselves trapped once waves pushed over the beach road. A few stayed because they wanted to "protect their property," and others said they stayed for the thrill of it. Some who rode out the storm in their elevated homes described the ordeal of listening to the thundering surf break under their feet. They felt their cottages shake and heard the waves wash through their ground-floor garages.

Human tragedy abounded. A Marine lance corporal drowned after the car in which he was riding over the high-rise bridge to North Topsail Beach was swept into the sound. Two fellow passengers escaped. A 75-year-old Surf City woman in need of round-the-clock nursing refused to leave her mobile home as the storm approached. Fran demolished her home, left her floating on a mattress through the flooded marsh, and bombarded her with high winds and rain. Rescue workers found her still alive the following day and took her to a hospital. She died the next day of hypothermia.

After the storm, two Federal Emergency Management Agency search-and-rescue teams arrived with dogs and sophisticated listening devices to hunt for at least five missing people. One team had to be airlifted to the northern end of the island. There was no other way in.

Meanwhile, the wrecked houses and streets drew national media attention. The island was closed for about a month following Fran to allow cleanup. Day in and day out, large debris-removal trucks rumbled up and down the roads. About 200 homes in North Topsail Beach, 170 in Surf City, and 25 in Topsail Beach were demolished, according to newspaper reports. Both the Ocean City Pier and the Scotch Bonnet Pier were taken out.

When the towns officially reopened, workers first were replaced by looters and a new phenomenon: destruction gawkers. Out-of-town officers were brought in to create a larger police presence, and a number of looters were arrested. As for the gawkers, they were told kindly not to clog the roads. "This one lady is driving down the road and videotaping at the same time," Surf City police chief David Jones told the *Wilmington Star-News*. "I'm like, 'Lady, what are you doing?' Meanwhile, she's going about five miles an hour."

Hardest hit were the island's many easily flipped mobile homes. A demolition project manager brought in to supervise cleanup said many people told him they were not at all upset over the loss, even though almost a mile of mobile homes near the Scotch Bonnet Pier had been destroyed. "I don't know anybody that thinks it was a bad thing, except the people that lived there of course," the manager told the *Star-News* in January 1997. Likewise, one Surf City councilman told the paper the island would be better off because of the two hurricanes. "It's a touchy subject, but a lot of the eyesores are gone now. There's a lot that'll come back newer and nicer."

Cleanup would not be complete for some time, especially in the ecologically sensitive Intracoastal Waterway between the island and the mainland. An article in the *Star-News* 10 months after the hurricane noted that "the marshes have remained strewn with washing machines, refrigerators, air conditioners, propane tanks and hunks of houses," as well as smaller items. State and federal agencies argued whether trying to remove the items would be more damaging than leaving them. They finally decided to remove them, the feds picking up 90 percent of the $2 million cost.

The environment had taken a huge hit. Barnes wrote, "Heavy beach erosion had moved mountains of sand, wiping out what remained of the dunes and their fragile vegetation. So much construction debris, paper, plastic, glass, appliances and toxic household products was washed into the marsh or buried in the sand that the area might never be completely cleaned up. Local conservationist Jean Beasley was quoted in the *North Carolina Herpetological Society Newsletter* as saying that Topsail Island was 'an ecological disaster, with tons of treated lumber and untreated sewage in the ocean and sound, mosquito trucks spraying every night, and those snakes that had survived the storm being killed by the hundreds as they sought high ground. Every sea turtle nest on the island had been inundated.' "

It would take a long while to clean up Topsail Island after the storm.

It would take longer to clean up its image as a tourist destination.

Nine months after Fran, a segment on CBS *This Morning* delivered another hit. "There are two kinds of people left in Surf City—those who are still cleaning up and those who are getting out," a narrator said while shots of debris and For Sale signs were shown. Mosquitoes were said to be breeding in standing water; rats were flourishing in debris.

The report infuriated government and chamber-of-commerce officials, who the *Star-News* reported had demanded an on-air apology. The report seemed overstated—the footage was provided by a North Carolina affiliate that had found only one instance of rats—but CBS stood by its overall accuracy and refused to make an apology. The Topsail Island Association of Realtors responded by hiring a Charlotte marketing firm to try to repair the image of the battered barrier island. It began advertising, mostly to North Carolina, South Carolina, and Virginia. The theme: "Topsail's Back—Start Packing."

In time, of course, the tourists did return. And in what may be the ultimate irony, the hurricanes that nearly destroyed Topsail brought the island national attention.

"What Fran did, it made people aware Topsail was here," Doug Medlin says. When Hurricane Hazel had hit the island 42 years earlier, Topsail received little attention. This time, with Fran, the world seemed to know about Topsail. "When we got back . . . , I knew it was going to change." Medlin says he bought three pieces of property before it became too late. Prices already had gone up.

CHAPTER SEVEN

Topsail Beach

Godwin's Market *is around the corner, it seems, from almost anywhere in town.* The little grocery store arrived in 1949 and hasn't left. And has barely changed. Anywhere else, Godwin's would have been torn down long ago, an unwanted reminder of simpler times and small-town provincialism. Progress would have overtaken it, replacing it, perhaps, with a 7-Eleven or a Starbucks. Even on Topsail, it is surprising that it has not been replaced by a duplex.

It is a must-see. Godwin's stands, frozen, in Topsail Beach. You *can* go home again. Two period gas pumps still stand out front, sentries protected from the island winds by a second-story overhang. The front door, angled on the right-hand corner, welcomes the time traveler. Step inside the screen door and you go back half a century.

Arrayed before you are just three aisles, flanked by rows of original wooden shelving. There has been no need to update on Topsail. The wooden checkout counter is to your immediate right. Most likely, Bill Godwin will be there, seated on a stool. This is as much Bill Godwin's conversation counter as checkout counter. Bill or his wife, Mary, has been seated there most business hours for more than three decades now, just as Bill's dad, J. A. Godwin, sat there for more than a quarter-century before that. What's your pleasure? Milk? Soap? Talking about the weather? Local goings-on?

Butch Parrish is the mayor of Topsail Beach, perhaps the most small-town of Topsail's three small towns. He may have as good an idea as anyone about the allure of the island. He says it all goes back to the idea of innocence.

The mayor's wife, Margaret, a longtime Topsailian, remembers being able to drive at age 12. There was so little on Topsail, what was she going to hit? She remembers her father, Edgar Waller, loading a lost turtle into the back of his Jeep and taking it to the beach to release it. Occasionally, Skip Rackley, the police chief in the 1950s, would slaughter a turtle and fix turtle soup for the townspeople.

Turtles are protected now, and children can no longer get away with driving at 12. But while his own children were growing up, Butch Parrish says, they were free to walk the town. There simply was no danger. Parents would drop their children at the miniature golf course—everyone in town called it "the Putt-Putt," though Putt-Putt franchise holders no doubt would have quibbled. Then the parents would simply drive off. "We'd leave the money with the operator," Parrish says. "He'd have all these stacks of money with names." There may be no more quintessential small-town image. "Nobody had any fears about leaving six-year-old children unattended," he says.

Times elsewhere have changed, and surely they have on Topsail Island as well. But it doesn't often seem like it. "It still has the feel of innocence," Parrish says. "That's part of the allure. Our crime is almost nil."

The Mayberry comparison is apt, Parrish says. "Small towns really are like that." People still trust one another. They talk to one another. "Small-town America. We know what's going on with each other." That can be disconcerting to newcomers on the island. Parrish laughs. "They have no idea that everything you say is repeated by everybody and heard by everybody and interpreted by everybody."

Navigate those small minefields, though, and you are rewarded. "It's an ability to feel completely untouched by all the stuff that goes on in the outside world," Parrish says. "You're in a little Garden of Eden here."

A newcomer senses that, wraps himself in it, and sometimes stays.

Jeffrey Stewart Price is the owner of the Beach Shop and Grill in Topsail Beach, one of Parrish's favorites. One of everyone's favorites. Old-timers still refer to it as "the Soda Shop" or "Warren's Soda Shop" or, if they knew Bill Warren, who started the shop in August 1952, as "Bill Warren's Soda Shop." It was one of the early businesses, arriving not long after the grocery store.

Warren's was a meeting place for vacationers of all ages. They might come for a sundae or a milk shake and stay to talk. At night, families would retire to their beach cottages or motel rooms and leave the shop to the younger set. "At nine o'clock," Price says, "the teens would court each other." Romances were started, nourished, and no doubt sometimes ended. Many an island teen worked at the shop as well during the summer. You can scarcely find a Topsail Beach native who doesn't want to share summer stories of working at Warren's or the Beach Shop and Grill. They bring a smile to the teller's face.

The early days were in a rented building on Anderson Boulevard. In 1959, the soda shop moved two blocks north to its present location at the corner of Anderson and Davis Avenue, where a gift shop was added. You can't go wrong with a gift shop on Topsail. There are three now—including The Gift Basket and Island Treasures—at this intersection alone, all of them popular. The Blue Gecko, a stylish gift shop and restaurant, is nearby, as is Quarter Moon Books and Gifts, a quaint yellow building worth anybody's time.

Anderson Boulevard is the town's main street.

The title "boulevard" speaks to Topsail's quaintness. Anderson Boulevard is merely a two-lane road, often sand strewn, carrying a 25-mile-an-hour speed limit in this part of town. It requires slowing down for flip-flop-wearing visitors who meander across it. Hardly the stuff of boulevards. But behind the Beach Shop, one block east and separated from the ocean by only dunes and a last row of homes, lies another boulevard, Ocean Boulevard, which is even smaller. A block the other way is Carolina Boulevard. Two blocks away is Channel Boulevard. Those are the only four north-south roads—each a two-lane "boulevard" the size of a subdivision street—in this part of the island. Elsewhere, there are fewer roads. Indeed, Ocean Boulevard disappears just one block north of Davis, where the island begins to narrow, leaving three roads. The supposed boulevard confronts a dead-end barrier and gives up.

The "Anderson" part of Anderson Boulevard honors the early developer of this end of the island, J. G. Anderson. A native of Pender County, he made his fortune in Florida, then moved back home, buying acreage enough for more than 300 homes on the island. Together with his son,

The New Topsail Market was only the third building on the south end of the island when it opened in 1949. Two men from Fayetteville, Bill Bland and J. A. Godwin, arrived on Topsail to open the market for fishermen. Though it has been rebuilt after storm damage, Godwin's New Topsail Market has remained largely unchanged despite the island's growth.

J. G. Anderson, Jr., he began building New Topsail Beach in 1949, long before there was an official town of Topsail Beach. He also opened the Breez-way Inn and Café in old military buildings; the Breezeway Motel and Restaurant continues today as an island mainstay.

The late Lewis Orr, who built what would become the Jolly Roger Inn and Pier, remembered Anderson and three other businessmen moving up from Florida to buy a huge portion of what is now Topsail Beach. "I understand they bought it for $40,000. In those days, that was a lot of money, of course," Orr said in a 2001 recorded interview. "I remember Mr. Anderson saying he would sell one lot [alone] down here one day for more than $40,000. We've seen that prophecy come true. To go back a little further than that, in 1912, Mr. Bridges from Wilmington and a partner came up here. Now, they had bought [from] where Topsail Motel is to the inlet for $2,500. So you can see how property values have increased up here."

A 1951 article in *The State* magazine said Anderson was proudly building "one of the most popular and fastest growing coastal resort towns on the South Atlantic." More than $1.5 million had been invested in the fledgling New Topsail Beach resort, and more than 100 homes and numerous commercial buildings were already up. Twenty apartments were on the way, along with 50 more homes. "There are stores, school buses, daily mail service, telephone service, fine drinking water, community church and many other facilities which makes for completeness of the modern town, at New Topsail Beach." Further, "due to its location, New Topsail Beach is said to be the most accessible beach resort to the most of North Carolina than any other."

If so, the other beaches must have been accessible only by parachute. Topsail Island has always been out of the way, despite what some promoters might claim. And as for the thriving resort town described in the article, New Topsail Beach, which would be incorporated as Topsail Beach in 1963, never did become more than a small town. Back in the early days, it wasn't even that.

Robin Orr was born in 1956, two years after his father, Lewis, built the pier. "There was really nobody down here at this end of the island when I was young," Orr says. The school bus would make a stop or two in Topsail Beach and a stop or two in Surf City, then head onto the mainland. Topsail Beach was not so much a town as a series of outposts. Even now, as the island's only town without a bridge, Topsail Beach can seem isolated. There are no accidental visitors. People who arrive at the little town stuffed down at the south end of the island don't do so by chance.

Topsail Beach was incorporated in 1963, when Robin Orr was seven. His father became the first mayor. Robin credits the town's founding fathers, like his dad, J. G. Anderson, builder-developer Tom Humphrey—whose son Bobby has been a mainstay on the town's board—and store owner J. A. Godwin. "They all had a vision for growth and development without overwhelming" the island and its character. Thus, even as Topsail Beach has grown, its essence has remained constant. "The mood of the place hasn't changed," Orr says. "It's still special. It's still family oriented." Part of that is location. "We're remote enough but easy enough to get to. . . . It's still unique."

Orr has lived here all his life.

Jeffrey Stewart Price, meanwhile, is a "come-here" who simply stumbled into all this.

Price was in the food business, making deliveries, and the Beach Shop was one of his customers. The magic of Topsail and of this little breakfast-and-lunch café took hold. Soon, the timing was right. "The guy who owned it had burned out," Price says. So he bought the old shop. It changed his life. Price knows what he has now, both in the shop and on the island. If not, there are continual reminders. "The old knotty pine," he says, looking up at the ceiling, "is how beach cottages were built back then." The pine ceilings that give the restaurant its distinctive look have been there since the 1960s, Price says. They will be there a good deal longer.

Price's first season was the summer of 2002. Almost immediately, he made a mistake. He laughs about it now, a little. Change does not come easily to Topsail, and Price made a change. "I left lunch items off the dinner menu, and I had to put them back," he says with a lesson-learned look. "I learned I still needed to have sandwiches so the kids could eat."

Another change worked, though. The shop had closed at two every afternoon, when the lunch crowd departed. Price added dinner during the summer months. Sales, he says, went through the roof. That first summer, he worked 16- or 17-hour days, and the business brought in $375,000. Now, it is up to $900,000 and rising.

The 21st century has brought boom times to the island—a mixed blessing, some would say. More and more visitors hear of Topsail's magic. More come for the water and the beach and stop in the shops and restaurants. More come for a week or two in the summer and decide to stay. Another home goes up.

Even nature seems to have given the boom a hand. "The shoulders of the season are getting broader and broader," Price says. He means Topsail no longer goes into hibernation after Labor Day, sleeping through the fall, winter, and spring before awakening in time for Memorial Day and the return of the visitors. "The seasons are getting milder," he says with conviction, as if ruling out mere wishful thinking. "It may be 70 degrees in December."

The best time to visit the island may well be the fall. Allan Libby, president of the area's chamber of commerce, has long maintained it is. Crowds are down, but the weather is as good as ever. Visitors can still swim in the ocean. Even in late fall, they can wade. There's still the ocean breeze. The shops. The people. The weather. The sound. The beach. The fishing.

One of Topsail Beach's best events, in fact, is Autumn With Topsail, put on the third weekend in October by the Topsail Island Historical and Cultural Arts Council. The event began in 1988 as a fund-raiser for the Assembly Building, which now houses the Missiles and More Museum, a small but first-rate facility that opened in 1997. Autumn With Topsail also serves as a season-stretcher for this little town, much the way the Miss America Pageant once stretched the season a week beyond Labor Day for Atlantic City. Visitors return. Residents come out. Topsail Beach shops are still open. Even the Topsail turtles—the island's premier attraction—are on display at the nearby turtle hospital. The turtles have been in "hibernation" from the public since the summer season ended. They come out for this weekend encore.

Always, the past is present at Topsail Beach.

Godwin's Market, practically right around the corner from the turtles, may be the prime example. The store came down from Bill Godwin's father, J. A. Godwin, known as "Averon" to friends and family. Averon's partner, Bill Bland, arrived from their hometown of Fayetteville, North Carolina, to build the store in 1949. "It was the third building at this end of the island," Bill Godwin says. "When there were two houses, Bill Bland said, 'We need a store.' "

Bland and the elder Godwin ran what was called the New Topsail Market jointly for a few summers, catering mostly to fishermen. By 1950, Bland wanted Godwin to run the store while he stayed in Fayetteville. Godwin moved down, eventually his family moved down, and later he bought the store outright. Averon's wife, Esther, found the life on Topsail lonely. The storms were worrisome and even frightening. For young Bill, it was intolerably lonely. "It was a huge shock to me, growing up in Fayetteville," the younger Godwin says now. "I was nine years old, in the Cub Scouts and in the YMCA. I had plenty of friends. There was nobody here." Going to school required a long bus ride to Hampstead on the mainland. A round-trip meant three hours on the bus each day. Godwin's older brother and sister seemed to adjust to the isolation more easily. "I grew to love nature," Godwin

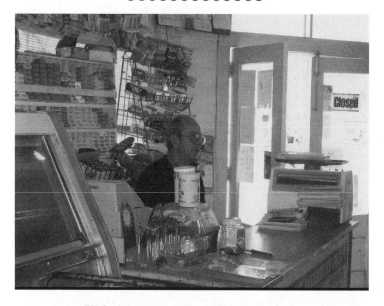

Bill Godwin greets shoppers from the original wooden counter just inside the front door. "In the summer, I sell a lot of bread, milk, soft drinks," the second-generation owner says. "My job is to figure out what people are going to run out of or what they forgot to bring. And I love the people coming in and talking."

says. "Between here and Surf City, there was nothing but woods."

Godwin got off the island as soon as he could, attending classes for a year at East Carolina University before taking the United States Navy up on its invitation to "Join the Navy and See the World." Near the end of his four-year stint, he met his future wife, Mary, in Boston. He returned home, this time with Mary, this time ready to accept it. "I found out I could respect Topsail now. I'd seen the rest of the world. There were things about Topsail no one else had." He returned to ECU to get a mechanical engineering degree, then went to work for Western Electric for six years. In the summers, he helped his dad run the store. When his father died in 1976, Bill wanted to come back and operate the store. Bill and Mary moved into an apartment upstairs from his mother, Esther.

Meanwhile, the Godwins bought a home for their retirement. They couldn't afford to live in it, instead renting it out to make mortgage payments. "I was lucky enough to buy an oceanfront home in '77," Godwin says with a smile. The six-bedroom home cost only $52,000, a price that seems comical now that oceanfront properties sell for seven figures. But paying off the five-year mortgage took all the Godwins' resources, all their time, all their energy. They were lucky to get a short vacation each year.

The store has been their life—even more so since Esther died in 1995. The name is still Godwin's New Topsail Market, but few use the "New Topsail" part of it. Often, it is just "Godwin's."

As Bill Godwin talks, a steady stream of customers comes in from the Autumn With Topsail festival. Children buy candy. A man buys a toothbrush. Another man asks for orange juice. Godwin asks if he wants large, medium size, or just a single drink, directing him to the back of the store when he hears the answer.

"How many family beaches do you know that are left on the East Coast?" Godwin continues. He says the lack of commercialization can be laid to two things others might say are "missing." First, there's no bridge on the southern end of the island. Second, there's no sewer system, meaning, in essence, the size of buildings is regulated by the limitations of septic tanks. Add to that Topsail's relative isolation—"You got to want to be here to find it"—and it's easy to see why development has lagged 30 years behind other beach towns.

Retirement still awaits, though Bill admits that working the store is more his desire than Mary's. The Godwins could make far more by selling. "The last couple of years, people

have come in and asked, 'When are you going to retire?' "
Godwin says. He tired of the question and found a response.
"I said, 'The first guy who comes by with $1 million cash and
lays it on the counter can have this place.' " That would keep
buyers away, unless one was crazy enough to actually offer $1
million.

Almost immediately, someone offered $900,000. The God-
wins turned it down. Mary suggested his asking price was too
low. Each year, he bumps it higher: $1.2 million, $1.5 million
. . . So far, the developers have refused. That suits Bill Godwin just fine. His store, he knows, is a good fit with Topsail.
Topsail is a good fit with him. "This is not my job. It's my
lifestyle."

The store is open from Easter to Thanksgiving, offering
full hours during the summer. "In the summer, I sell a lot of
bread, milk, soft drinks. My job is to figure out what people
are going to run out of or what they forgot to bring. And I
love the people coming in and talking."

He pauses. "I don't run a convenience store. This is more
like the old-timey grocery store," he says.

Could there be any other kind in Topsail Beach?

A woman comes in and buys milk and eggs. Bill Godwin
rings up her purchases, exchanges small talk with her, and re-
turns with a smile, well aware the point has just been made.

CHAPTER EIGHT

Surf City

*T*opsail Island, like the quintessential small
town, has only one traffic light. The light, in
the town of Surf City, greets visitors who
venture a few blocks onto the island.

But not many small towns have a swing
bridge.

That iconic old dark green swing bridge
leading onto the island at Surf City has become as much a symbol of Topsail as the lone
light and the white-sand beach and the fishing piers and the quaint shops and even the
old missile towers.

Sooner or later, while they enter or leave
the island, everyone gets caught by the swing
bridge. The bridge opens on the hour, less often if boat traffic is thin. In summer, that's
enough to back up automobile traffic at least
a mile and a half onto the mainland. Experienced vacationers know not to arrive on

The ornate green swing bridge at Surf City has been carrying visitors onto and off the island for more than 50 years. The eye-catching bridge rotates 90 degrees to open for boats to pass. It is one of only a few swing bridges remaining on the East Coast.

the island with a gas tank on empty. They may end up calling a tow truck and trying to avoid the angry looks of other drivers.

A driver's temptation is to become annoyed at the delay. Better to consider it an opportunity. Let the pace of Topsail begin to wash over the soul. No one's in a hurry on Topsail—or if they are, it's not for long. A driver may as well begin relaxing. And watching the bridge.

This is a step back in time. Topsail's swing bridge was born in a more intricate age—the handiwork, it seems, of someone playing with a giant Erector Set and a sense of whimsy. It is unique. It is complex. The first time drivers are signaled to a stop and the two warning gates are lowered, they may unconsciously look skyward. The center of the bridge should open upward.

It does not. Instead, the bridge begins to move.

The whole bridge.

The whole bridge moves!

Drivers have a chance to get out, walk nearer, and take a

It takes eight minutes for the 127-foot-long bridge to swing perpendicular to the road, allow a boat through, and swing all the way closed. The bridge opens on the hour unless no boats are waiting.

look. And a picture. There will be more than enough time to get back to their parked cars. The opening and closing take eight minutes. The bridge begins slowly, ever so slowly, to rotate. It swings 90 degrees into position, perpendicular to the roadway, so boats can pass.

The two-story metal-deck bridge is 127 feet long, according to Surf City town clerk Patti Arnold. (The entire bridge structure is 463 feet from roadway edge to roadway edge.) It is staffed 24 hours a day.

It is now, and always has been, a marvel. The bridge replaced a pontoon structure left on the island by the military, which itself needed to be temporarily replaced after Hurricane Hazel took it out in 1954. The much-awaited modern $432,000 swing span opened the next year to a celebration. Hundreds gathered on Saturday, November 5, 1955, to see what newspapers called both the "Surf City Bridge" and the "Pender County Bridge." The first traffic passed over it after dedication speeches by what newspapers described as both "a number of" and "many" highway and government officials and, of course, the ceremonial cutting of a blue-and-white ribbon by Lynia Blossom, Miss Pender County 1956. A seafood dinner described as "delicious" was served afterward.

Now more than half a century old and a traffic problem, the bridge is due for replacement. Surf City mayor Zander Guy says that probably won't happen before 2015. Many, including Guy, are opposed to changing the bridge's design because they feel it captures the character of the island. No one will be surprised, then, if the new bridge looks something like the original. Whenever it is built, the new bridge almost surely will be higher. Only tall boats will require it to open. And it almost surely will be a drawbridge, so openings will go more quickly.

But a new bridge won't swing perpendicular to the road.

Take the pictures now.

If the swing bridge is the main entrance to the island of Topsail, in many ways the lone traffic light is the center.

Whereas the town of Topsail Beach to the south became home to vacationers, the site of more seasonal homes, Surf City became the hub of the island, says Mayor Guy. The reason is simple enough. Surf City grew up in the middle of the island, across from what was Topsail's only bridge for years and is still its easiest access.

The oldest of Topsail Island's three towns, Surf City is also the only one with more than a handful of businesses. Indeed, it has many more than a handful. There are gift shops, clothing shops, restaurants, a grocery store, a gas station—all within a few blocks of the traffic light.

In most places, old buildings have accommodated the new nicely. In the middle of town, an IGA grocery and several gift shops occupy what was the island's earliest shopping center.

Yet just down the road, for instance, was the modern Topsail Internet Café. That café is gone now. The old shops remain.

Across the street from the IGA is the newer Topsail Art Gallery and Frame Shop, one of several galleries on the island doing a brisk business with tourists and newcomers. Seascapes and nautical themes abound. Diane Masi, a local artist working in the shop, says many customers are decorating new homes and not necessarily looking for Topsail landmarks. But a good many do look for the swing bridge, the island's piers, and a variety of Topsail ocean, sound, and beach scenes. Artists like Sam McLaughlin, Lloyd Childers, and David Lewis either paint the island, live on it, or both. Enlarged photographs of Topsail are another favorite. No photographer has a larger following than Conrad Pope of Wilmington, locally famous for his aerial shots of the island.

The ocean, the fishing pier, and Topsail's famed beach are only a short walk away. A walk the other way, to the inland side, leads to the striking Beach House Marina. Its two four-story, three-sided facilities can hold 192 boats in dry storage—at least until one is replaced by a planned resort. Another 25 boats can be kept in the water. Nearby are such Surf City mainstays as the Topsail Island Trading Company, the Iron Pelican, and Herring's Outdoor Sports.

The town's year-round population is less than 2,000, but tourists swell it to many times that in summer. What is striking as one walks around the town, then, is the relative absence of large shops, other than occasional T-shirt-and-souvenir-emporiums. Despite its growth, Surf City is no Myrtle Beach. "It never will be," Mayor Guy says. "I wish I could take the credit for that." It is the island's narrowness, he says, that precludes major commercial growth.

The town was incorporated in 1949, a year after the military left the island, when it was nothing more than a fishing village. There had been little population in the area that wasn't associated with the armed forces, Guy says. In the 1940s, Camp Davis and its German prisoner-of-war camp were based in nearby Holly Ridge. The military built a pontoon bridge that lasted until Hurricane Hazel. The big green building still standing in Surf City was the Army's motor-pool garage. Topsail Island, Guy adds with a local's pride, also had been "selected to be Cape Canaveral—but politics changed all that."

In the early 1950s, the year-round population still was only about 100. Guy has lived year-round on Topsail since 1990, but his family had a house on the island going back to 1950, when he was but two years old. "This basically was a gateway for people to come fish. Fishing was a real big pastime for people because they didn't have money to do other things."

Perhaps no one has seen more of Surf City than Doug Medlin.

Perhaps no one was less impressed with his first sight.

The year was 1952 and Medlin was four years old when his father moved the family to the island full-time and he first saw the Atlantic Ocean. Medlin laughs about it now. "When we walked up on the dune, I said, 'Is this as big as it is?' "

His father, Charlie Medlin, had been here when the island's first developer, Edgar Yow, named the town Surf City. This was long before Jan and Dean sang "Surf City," promising "two girls for every boy." The California duo's hit song of the 1960s gave the town a boost. People still ask if this is the place they were singing about.

Charlie Medlin became one of the early entrepreneurs in the infant town. Fishing came first in Surf City, but small businesses were a close second. Charlie opened the first icehouse on the island, the Coastal Ice Company, along with a bait-and-tackle shop. The icehouse was in the spot where

Doug Medlin now has his modern Fishing Village, between the swing bridge and the center of town. By 1956, Charlie Medlin was using the spot for a grocery store that became affiliated with IGA, the Independent Grocers Association.

The island has never had a large year-round population. Back in the 1950s, it was minuscule. In the mid-1950s, there were perhaps 15 civilian families and 15 to 20 military families on the island, Doug Medlin says. When he was in the first grade, there were only seven schoolchildren of any age. Before Hurricane Hazel, they were driven to Topsail School in Hampstead on the mainland. "After Hazel, we didn't have a bridge. So we met up at the post office, and they put us on one of those ducks, the amphibious vehicles," he says. As teenagers later, they would swim, fish, and play baseball. "I can remember when we could play a full game of baseball on the street and never move. That was Topsail Drive, and that was the only street on the island. There was no traffic." He laughs. "Of course, you couldn't get enough to play for a full team. You had three players on one side and three on the other side." Arcades were the thing then, and Pop's Arcade was the place to go. They also played miniature golf and went to the skating rink in Topsail Beach. Beyond that, the closest entertainment was a movie theater in Wilmington.

The town's architecture still had a distinct military look. Camp Davis had swelled the population of nearby Holly Ridge from 28 people to 110,000 during World War II, Medlin says. In the 1950s, the island had buildings from the large camp and from Operation Bumblebee. Hotels and apartments went into many of them. Medlin's church had been a military barracks. The officers' club would become Barnacle Bill's; a fishing pier would be added later. Two barracks remain today, Medlin adds. One is used for a motel, and the other is the back end of the Mainsail Restaurant.

During that first decade, Surf City was the smallest of small towns. J. B. Batts opened a fishing-tackle shop. Roland Batts, his brother, would be the town's mayor from the mid-1950s until the 1960s. There was a post office, a grocery store, and a café, Medlin says. Not much else. The Surf City Pier and then Barnacle Bill's Pier were both built in the 1950s.

Kenny Batts, owner of Batts' Grill, is one of J. B. Batts's four sons. "My father's family got a Queen's Grant for the property from the queen of England," Kenny explains. In colonial days, the English crown awarded land on the island and the nearby mainland. The Batts grant was roughly a mile wide, stretching from the island to about where U.S. 17 runs on the mainland, Kenny says. It was his great-grandfather who was given the land, but he did no building on the island. "Really, they kept cattle over there."

J. B.'s oldest son, James Batts, born in 1948, remembers his dad building in the 1950s. "He had what he called a construction company. Really, he hauled dirt and installed septic tanks." But the elder Batts also built a couple of fishing-tackle shops, a motel, and oceanfront cottages. "Another thing that helped get the place developed was that he built the campground. Now, people had a place to live." The Batts family since has run half a dozen island campgrounds for trailers.

Others were in on the growth. Medlin remembers Al Ward building a shopping center with a new IGA store and a few shops in the late 1950s and 1960s. "At the time, that was a *big* shopping center." Ward was the island's first developer. Indeed, the sign outside the Ward Realty Corporation office proclaims, "Original Developers of Topsail Island." Ward was also a town commissioner and public-works director when Surf City was incorporated.

No one was more instrumental at the start, though, than Edgar Yow, a Wilmington attorney, developer, and visionary.

Doug Medlin, owner of the Fishing Village shops, has been living on Topsail since 1952. He was four years old when his family moved to the island and he saw the Atlantic Ocean. "When we walked up on the dune, I said, 'Is this as big as it is?' " He has since come to think more highly of the ocean view.

"Edgar Yow was sort of the one they looked up to," Medlin says. Yow hastened the conversion of Topsail from a military island to a civilian one, bought land, and lined up developers. It was he who gave Surf City its name. It was also he who, at the same time, organized the development of Ocean City on Topsail—the only place on the North Carolina coast where black people could own property at the time, Medlin notes. In any discussion of Surf City's early history, he says, Yow, Batts, and Ward deserve primary mention.

The Medlins deserve mention, too. It was Doug Medlin's grandfather who bought a 50-foot-wide oceanfront lot in Surf City, Doug says. The love of salt water was passed down. "My father liked the allure of the island. He liked the fishing, the ocean. He saw it as a growing opportunity." Charlie Medlin bought Paradise Pier, six miles north of his grocery store, in 1963. Not long after the sale, the pier burned down. He sold the property, then bought Barnacle Bill's Pier, just one mile from the store.

"We had Barnacle Bill's until Hurricane Fran decided she wanted it" in 1996, Doug Medlin says. Instead of rebuilding it, the younger Medlin broke ground on the family's original site, by then a fish-and-tackle shop. Medlin turned it into the Fishing Village, a collection of well-appointed shops selling everything from fishing gear to clothing to real estate.

Maintaining at least some of the character of the tiny island while facing the inevitable development is the concern of nearly everyone in public life on Topsail Island. Nowhere is this more of a political balancing act than in Surf City. Not only are small period beach cottages at risk of being swallowed up, so, too, are quaint throwback businesses.

Walk the streets of Surf City and see them: Batts' Grill, the IGA supermarket, the Surf City Pharmacy, the Ward Realty Corporation office, Guy's own real-estate office, Mollie's Restaurant, the Loggerhead Motel, Tiffany's Motel, and dozens of others. In most towns, they would be gone already.

Growth has begun and most certainly will continue on the mainland. Surf City is expanding off the island as parts of Pender County seek to be annexed, primarily to gain water and sewer lines. National chains most likely will end up along these stretches of S.R. 210 and S.R. 50 out to U.S. 17 and beyond. Off-island growth began as long ago as 1993, when a Food Lion grocery store opened on S.R. 210. Gift shops like the popular Docksider Gifts and Shells are here, too. More recent Surf City expansion has started an even larger boom, led by the opening of a Lowe's home-improvement warehouse in 2006.

Batts' Grill is one of the first—and one of the oldest—buildings visitors see after crossing onto Topsail Island. The no-frills restaurant is owned by one of the sons of J. B. Batts, an early island developer who built on land his family was granted by the queen of England.

In addition to that geographic oddity, Surf City deals with a political oddity. Thanks to one of its earlier annexations, the town is actually located in two counties. About 70 percent of the population resides in Pender County and the remainder in Onslow County, to the north. That can be a headache for those who don't realize that their 911 emergency calls will be handled by an Onslow dispatcher or that an ambulance will take them to an Onslow hospital, farther away than other Surf City residents have to travel. Mayor Guy adds that about 720 homes are connected to Onslow's water system, which turns off the water for approaching storms. When that happens, he says, his phone rings off the hook.

Guy, in the real-estate business since 1970, is aware enough of his surroundings to appreciate them, savvy enough to make a living off them. Politics has been in his blood even longer, no doubt from the day he was born. His father served in the

North Carolina Senate. Guy himself was mayor of Jacksonville before moving to Surf City. The two jobs—real estate and politics—appear a natural fit on Topsail Island, where every third person seems to be selling real estate. "*Politician*," Guy says, "means *salesman*." He makes a convincing case. Everyone has something to sell, he says, whether it's a plot of land, an idea, or oneself. His job is to make the sale fit.

In buying the land for Soundside Park, Surf City both took property that developers would have wanted and, says Guy, alienated many by displacing a mobile-home park. Mobile homes have been a part of Surf City since the beginning—an eyesore to some, an example of Topsail's opportunity to others—but their numbers have dwindled as more money has come to the island. Shortly after becoming mayor in 1999, Guy helped put together a deal for the 19 exquisite acres that would become Soundside Park. The land, bought for $1.5 million in 1999, was worth $15 million just six years later. Many park users would say it's worth far more than that.

Likewise, the town's announcement in early 2006 that it was buying nearly two acres of prime property, encompassing 160 oceanfront feet, may have disheartened developers. The town needed the land for parking. Places to leave a car or truck are at a premium anywhere near Surf City's center.

Thus far, Surf City's balancing act has kept the town at least within shouting distance of its roots. "We've had our share of growth like everybody else," James Batts says. "But basically, it's still a family-type beach. Just more people."

But change inevitably has come. Doug Medlin remembers the first time his family ever locked the door. It was when he was 16 and the family got wind of a local break-in. "We were going to be gone a couple of weeks at Christmas. . . . But even after that, the only time you locked it was if you were going to be gone a long time."

The Beach House Marina was built with two four-story facilities to hold up to 192 boats, alongside another 25 in the water.

That quaint innocence continues. Medlin laughs, remembering a recent call. It seems a businessman had left his door unlocked, then gone off to Wilmington. Medlin called the businessman. Was there anything he wanted Medlin to do? "He said, 'I don't know. Maybe go take the money out of the register.'"

From time to time, there is talk of removing Surf City's lone stoplight, symbolic or not. The feeling is that the island's summer traffic actually might be better controlled without it.

But the talk is usually talked down. As silly as it sounds to have just one traffic light, think what it would be like to have none at all.

And then there is the green swing bridge—too narrow, too low, too slow. Too obsolete.

Odds are as a visitor leaves the island he or she will cross that swing bridge, leaving Topsail behind for another week, another year, or perhaps forever. Odds are the bridge will be open to traffic—it usually is, after all—and the visitor will be able to zip right across on the way off the island.

Odds are by now he'll wish it weren't.

CHAPTER NINE

Ocean City

Caronell Chestnut's *first view of Topsail Island, in 1950, brought a scowl to her face.* She looked out on the acres of empty oceanfront property near the middle of the island. She had just arrived with her husband, Wade, and together they would become the first family at the new "black beach." Her husband was one of the beach's developers.

"There were no homes when I went there to look at it," she would say years later. "We often laughed about it because I could see no vision like he could. He said, 'This will be the residential area, and this will be the business area,' and so on. I could see nothing but sky and land and water. I saw nothing else." It took a long time before she bought into his dream.

The area was Ocean City Beach, and it was developed on land owned by Wilmington lawyer Edgar A. Yow. Previously, black people could not buy ocean property in North Carolina. The only beach in the area where blacks could go was Seabreeze, just north of Carolina Beach. Seabreeze was not even on the ocean.

Topsail was being opened to private development—the rest of it white—after years of use by the military. The sole access was a floating pontoon bridge across the Intracoastal Waterway at the new town of Surf City. As for nearby Ocean City, just to the north of Surf City, only parts of it had street-lights, decent roads, and electricity.

Drive along the main road, Island Drive, in what is to-day North Topsail Beach and you can still see the vestiges of this historic area. Ocean City now seems little different from its immediate surroundings. There are few markings to sug-gest otherwise. Most notable is the now-ravaged fishing pier, restaurant, and tackle shop that Wade Chestnut built. The structure encompassed and expanded what had been one of the Operation Bumblebee towers. Alongside the main road directly across from the ocean tower is a small, unused Episco-pal chapel, the Wade H. Chestnut Memorial Chapel.

Caronell Chestnut died in 2002 at age 86, a much-honored civic leader in both Wilmington and Topsail. But she had told her and her husband's story in an interview with Dianne Adjan Logan of CreatiVideo, Inc., for a commercial videotape about Topsail Island. That videotape is now in the State Ar-chives of North Carolina.

Yow first took his idea to Dr. Samuel J. Gray, a Wilmington physician, who contacted the owners of an automobile business he patronized. Wade Chestnut sold his share of the business to his two brothers and dove into the Topsail project.

Many blacks, though, were skeptical of the "opportunity" to buy into the one-mile beach area. "You see, in 1949, these were the days of segregation," Caronell Chestnut told Logan.

Though battered by storms and now standing vacant, this former restaurant remains the most visible symbol of the historic Ocean City area. In 1949, when blacks could not buy ocean property in North Carolina, Wade Chestnut helped open the mile-long beach area to them. His restaurant incorporated a deserted missile tower. He built an attached fishing pier later. The complex became a focal point of the community.

"So blacks were a little hesitant about putting money into property like that because they didn't know if it was a gimmick or whether it would go or just what. As time went on, with a lot of advertising and a lot of meetings that my husband would attend where blacks assembled to try to interest them, it started off, well, slowly."

Wade Chestnut had quickly opened a restaurant in Tower 6. He needed a place to sleep, so his home was built first. Caronell, a teacher, stayed in Wilmington with their young sons, joining him on weekends and in the summer.

When she came down, Caronell hosted gatherings for potential buyers in their Ocean City home. Lots began to sell, slowly. "They were so cheap in those early years. You could get a lot for $500 or $1,000 on the oceanfront. I mean, very, very inexpensive." Soon, Mother Nature stepped in. "Just as we were beginning to get people's confidence to begin building, then Hurricane Hazel came along. When this happened, we had to start over from day one almost. Then of course money was very scarce. It was a sacrifice for even people who made good salaries. It was a sacrifice to invest in a second home." Virtually all of the 15 to 20 homes were destroyed. "We lost our home completely because we did not build on pilings. We just built on the ground, just a regular building as they were built. We finally learned the hard way." Like those elsewhere on Topsail, Ocean City homeowners began rebuilding. A few homes could be repaired. Most had to be rebuilt from scratch.

Meanwhile, the Chestnuts held Sunday church services in their living room. They were led by a visiting priest, the Reverend Edwin Kirton of St. Mark's Episcopal Church in Wilmington, whom the Chestnuts invited every summer. "Everybody came with their folding chairs. You'd see them coming across the dunes to the service," Chestnut said. That was the beginning of the community's chapel. A permanent building put up in 1957 would be named for her husband after his death. Wade Chestnut also began hosting children for two weeks each summer in a 10-room motel he helped build. That led to permanent Episcopal children's camps on the mainland.

Later in the 1950s, Wade and the other developers constructed Ocean City's fishing pier. Immediately, the community's traffic increased. Blacks now had a pier they could use. "Of course, now that things have changed, they can go to any fishing pier they like, but that was the beginning of it. Even that [Ocean City] fishing pier now is integrated," Chestnut said. Unfortunately, the year after the interview, 1996, Hurricane Fran took down the Ocean City Pier. It has not been rebuilt.

Wade Chestnut died in 1961, "just as we were getting things going, we thought, very well," his widow told Logan. The community continued. "One of the things that we stressed is we didn't want any rowdiness nor frivolity or what-not around." Children needed to feel safe. The community association adopted a rule forbidding children from going into the ocean without an adult. "Very often, the children would go from house to house: 'Will you stand out so we can go into the water?' "

By the late 1980s, about 100 families lived in Ocean City. Through the years, the community had grown close, gathering for annual picnics, fish frys, and oyster roasts.

Going crabbing was a community event, too. Crab gumbo became locally famous. "When we first moved there, crabs were just everywhere," Chestnut said. "You could just go down to the water and catch them two or three on the line at one time. But the best place to crab was at the [north] end of the island, where the St. Regis is now." The road didn't go that far, of course. The families would drive as far as they could, park their cars, then take off walking a mile or so across the dunes, bushel baskets in hand, to reach the spot. "If you would go just as the tide was changing, you couldn't get the crabs off the lines fast enough. One of the tales my son often tells is that we filled all the bushel baskets, the crabs were still biting, and we didn't want to leave. He says I asked him to take off his jeans, and we tied the ends of the jeans so we could put more crabs in there."

Edgar Yow's decision to integrate the island had not been popular during the time of segregation, Chestnut told the *Wilmington Star-News* in 1995. "But he was a fine man, and many admired him for it, too."

There was some resentment initially toward blacks and Yow, she admitted to Logan. "You could see a little vandalism in the very beginning. There was a little resistance. In fact, Mr. Yow was greatly criticized for having done what he did. In spite of that, he did it out of the kindness of his heart. I understand whatever money was invested there, he had been offered twice the amount to give up that idea. But he did not do it. He was a fine man." Chestnut declined a chance to criticize the segregationists, saying only, "We just have to forgive them. They didn't realize."

Long after Wade Chestnut died, services continued to be held at the Wade H. Chestnut Memorial Chapel every summer Sunday. Whites and blacks attended together.

CHAPTER TEN

North Topsail

In the fall of 2005, Loraine Carbone, the North Topsail Beach town clerk, set herself up in the town manager's office. That was her prerogative. She was, after all, also the interim town manager. More than that, though, it was fortuitous. Having two offices is no longer a luxury when one is damaged by a hurricane.

Carbone could be a case study for North Topsail Beach. She reflects both the background and the unbridled joy of many who live or work or vacation in Topsail Island's newest town, and she's seen the difficulties, too. Carbone and her husband are transplanted northeasterners who decided to move south from Connecticut in 1993, though it might have been a decision made for them by the 92 inches of snow that fell that winter. They had visited Myrtle Beach, South Carolina, which was fine for vacations but not, they knew, a place they wanted to live. They set up an appointment instead with a real-estate agent in Wilmington.

The night before the appointment, they stopped in a pizza place in Wilmington. A small newspaper on a waiters' table caught their eye. The headline: "The Best-Kept Secret in North Carolina: Topsail Island." Carbone remembers it contained advertisements for Topsail Beach, for Serenity Point at the south end of Topsail Beach, and for North Shore Country Club, just off the island's northern end at Sneads Ferry on the mainland.

They immediately canceled their appointment with the Wilmington agent.

The Carbones scheduled another appointment, 45 minutes to the north on Topsail Island. The agent there tried to sell them on Topsail Beach, but it hardly mattered. This was all glorious. They grew up on the beaches of Rhode Island. Those at Topsail were so beautiful. Loraine and her husband would decide on the country-club area off North Topsail Beach, just beyond the high-rise bridge that is one of two ways on and off the island (and just beyond the welcome sign announcing the town is the home of Miss North Carolina 2000). "The first year," Carbone says, "here we were walking on the beach in January. . . . I gave away my long winter coats."

The Carbones discovered what others would find in North Topsail: It is a family-oriented beach. It is not commercial in the slightest, yet there are small shops nearby in Surf City and larger ones in Wilmington and Jacksonville. What makes this place unique? "Not having any commercial district," she says. "It's just a quiet beach. The dolphins. The egrets. It's a place people like to come back to every year."

There are, of course, the hurricanes. Carbone remembers the horrors of Hurricanes Bertha and Fran in 1996, which

Building continues nonstop in beautiful North Topsail Beach
despite the threat of hurricanes and flooding. Striking homes are
being built for retirees, year-round residents, and vacationers alike.
They often dwarf cottages elsewhere on the island.

hit North Topsail Beach especially hard. "It was the island
war zone," she said. In 2005, Hurricane Ophelia, which damaged Carbone's town clerk's office and other parts of North
Topsail's government building, never made landfall. It simply
churned off the coast for days, bombarding the island with
high winds and then floodwaters. Following the storm, eight
duplexes at the extreme northern end stood in the water at
high tide. The town condemned those 16 homes, ordering
them torn down.

North Topsail Beach, on the whole, has the island's lowest

land, its official elevation only five feet above sea level. (Surf City is 21 feet above sea level and Topsail Beach 12 feet.) Moreover, North Topsail is especially narrow in some places. In other words, it is a dicey place to build, particularly along the ocean or the inlet on the north end of the island.

It has always been a dicey place to build.

In 1982, the federal government determined that structures should never have been built on seven miles of shore at the northern end. Under the Coastal Barrier Resources Act, federal flood insurance and most federal disaster aid would be available no longer.

In 1990, six geologists asked the North Carolina governor to halt development at North Topsail and asked the state's attorney general to investigate if real-estate developers there were committing fraud. "It is our opinion that the physical danger to inhabitants on North Topsail Island (north of the north bridge) has reached an unconscionable level," the six wrote. "This may be America's most dangerous development." Their legal clout was limited. But the geologists also hoped to educate the land-buying public about the combination of North Topsail's low elevation, narrow width, and unstable line of man-made dunes.

Storms are always an issue. So is erosion, especially at the northern end. The island keeps being eaten away. "We're hauling in sand," Carbone says, and she doesn't mean just a sandbox full. The town adds 58,000 cubic feet of sand to the beach at a time, as well as plantings.

Yet the building continues. The building accelerates. Homebuyers see the paradise that is North Topsail Beach and don't see—or don't want to see—how fragile it is. Their $1 million homes, their $2 million homes, could be underwater soon. They take that chance. They pay that price.

Carbone looks out her office window, toward the ocean.

Topsail's maritime forest of oaks and other vegetation serve multiple purposes. The gnarled oaks provide a unique beauty, a sense of balance, and, of course, summer shade. Moreover, the forest literally helps hold together the fragile island of shifting sand.

Nearly a dozen large homes have been built or are being built right here, with more on their way. "A lot of people are investing. See all those houses here," she says, gesturing to a large expanse of land between her office and the ocean. "Eight years ago, there was nothing. They're huge, *huge*. Five or six bedrooms. They're all to rent."

The town is a magnet for northerners, particularly from Delaware, New York, and New Jersey, Carbone says, and she can certainly understand that. It's a terrific place for a second home or a retirement home. Many people are even putting in swimming pools.

When the 2000 census was taken, North Topsail Beach had 844 full-time residents. Since then, the growth has been exponential. In 2000, permits were issued for 20 single-family homes and two duplexes. By 2004, the numbers were 127 and 16, an eightfold increase in just four years. By mid-2005, says Christina Watkins, the deputy town clerk, there were already 2,324 homes in the town—just homes, not people—including both residences and rental units. The growth continues, both on the island and off. The marina in Sneads Ferry, just on the other side of the Intracoastal Waterway, has been sold; a gated community is there now, Carbone notes. There is little sign of slowing. Demand is greater than the available real estate.

Loraine Carbone looks out one of the two windows in the town manager's office on the second floor of the government building. Life is not only good, it is beautiful. "It's like you're on water all the time," she says. "Just look out there. You've got the Intracoastal Waterway. You see the boats, especially the sailboats."

Moments later, she is at the other window. Beyond are the protective sand dunes and then the Atlantic Ocean. The view is breathtaking. Having a panorama like this is extraordinary. Having two seems beyond comprehension.

In Surf City and in Topsail Beach, a visitor can step out of the car and within five minutes, 10 at most, walk to nearly any business or landmark or attraction in town. There is a sense of community, of smallness even. Surf City and Topsail Beach both are towns—villages, really—in the old-fashioned sense. There is a center of town.

North Topsail Beach has as much an island-resort feel as a small-town feel. There is more open land and less commercial development. A small convenience store, a few restaurants, and a few resorts are all that might qualify. Instead, dozens of retail stores, a hotel, and a country club are across the highrise bridge at Sneads Ferry on the mainland. Seeing North

Topsail Beach takes a drive. A scenic drive it is, complete with ocean and dunes and $1 million homes. But one just doesn't walk anywhere, unless it's to the beach.

Heading north from Surf City, S.R. 210 turns from New River Drive into Island Drive, and the driver senses a difference. Beautiful homes become increasingly large by the mile. A few more miles and S.R. 210 turns left to the bridge to leave the island. Locals call it "the high-rise bridge" or sometimes "the high bridge" or even "the tall bridge." This turn in the road may be the symbolic center of North Topsail Beach. This is roughly the geographic center of town—here are the town hall and police station, after all—though the location is farther from the ocean than nearly any other spot in North Topsail.

It also signals a symbolic turn in the road. The driver wanting to continue northward on the island must leave this main road before it reaches the town hall. The turn is onto the only remaining northbound road, New River Inlet Road. Now, the road actually begins to *feel* lower. It is no illusion. The island here is barely above sea level—and during violent storms, sometimes below it.

On the right is the once-controversial Villa Capriani. The large luxury resort, which underwent an exterior face-lift in 2005-6, is one of the island's man-made gems. Everything from multibedroom villas to a multilevel courtyard with pools and a whirlpool is just feet from the beach. It is decidedly un-Topsailian in its scale, and rules were bent to build it, including the moving of the road to the interior side, allowing the Villa Capriani to become an oceanfront resort. But no one who passes doesn't pause to look. And few who stay at the resort fail to return one day.

Farther north is a mixture of new homes, old homes, condominiums, the Palm Tree Market convenience store, and the St. Regis Resort, the island's tallest structure, topped by The Atlantis Restaurant on the seventh floor. New River Inlet Road has run out now. To continue northward, one must make a couple of turns onto North Shore Drive—home of water-distressed houses—and River Road, which runs out at the beach.

At the beach, the island runs out, too.

The beach seems particularly quiet here on the northern edge. One can hear the ripples of the water and the calls of the birds. The beach here is the most vulnerable on the island, being worn away by the currents and the winds and, some say, government dredging that keeps open New River Inlet. Signs prohibit vehicles past a certain point. The beach can be nearly deserted, though almost always at least a few people come to this remote spot.

A dune, some sand, the water. Serenity. Solitude.

This end of the island may be falling into the sea. But it is understandable why people would want to be here until it does.

At six-foot-nine, Rodney Knowles strikes an imposing figure. He looks like a basketball player, and indeed he was, first at Davidson College, a national power under famed coach Lefty Driesell, then as a professional with the Phoenix Suns in the National Basketball Association. He was the town's first mayor, from 1990 to 1992, and has been back in the office since 2004.

Knowles remembers Topsail Island from visits to his father's summer cottage back in the late 1950s. It would be decades before he returned for good. When he did, it was in 1985, in what would become North Topsail Beach. At the time, the community was called West Onslow Beach, and little was there. The majority of homes were mobile homes.

This was virtually an outpost—almost inaccessible, essentially forgotten, it sometimes seemed. "It would take 45 minutes to two hours to get emergency calls answered," Knowles says. For developers, it must have seemed as lawless as the Wild West. "A lot of large condominiums were going up, and it seemed the county didn't care."

Newspaper clippings from the time show developers and officials both ran afoul of the law. One tells of a developer spending 15 months in prison on a contempt charge stemming from a lawsuit. Another reports building officials were unqualified under state law to inspect the high-rise buildings. Another says the Onslow County water system had insufficient pressure to fight fires on such buildings. Another passes along a 1988 study concluding that after proposed development was completed, it would take 15 to 19 hours to evacuate during a peak-season hurricane. Newspaper editorials during the 1980s and early 1990s railed against local officials who approved high-density building at the north end, where only one vulnerable road provided access.

But the image of a paradise persisted because it was so easy to see. A St. Regis Resort sales brochure in the late 1980s captured the allure of Topsail: "Imagine for one mystical moment, a vacation hideaway so untouched by bustling change, it doesn't appear on most maps. A secret island spot . . . where overcrowding is something only the birds understand along the 26 miles of crystal-coated beaches. Imagine your vacation home with a view of the water everywhere." It was all true, though there was no mention of any downside.

Knowles was a real-estate agent who saw the advantage of local people having input into how their area would develop. It was easy for locals to persuade him to head up an incorporation committee in 1988. That led to an official North Topsail Beach in 1990, with Knowles as the town's first mayor. Really,

Villa Capriani, constructed in the days before effective building codes in North Topsail Beach, is one of the island's few true resorts. It draws vacationers from up and down the East Coast. A beachside road was moved during its construction, allowing the site to become oceanfront property.

he says, it was about police protection, fire protection, trash collection, and the like, as well as limiting growth.

The twin hurricanes of 1996, Bertha and Fran, wiped out 400 homes, Knowles says. One-quarter of the town. "Next to me on either side, the homes were destroyed." North Topsail changed after the hurricane cleanup—not with fewer homes but with more. Prices took off about 1998 or 1999. Oceanfront property, once ranging from $150,000 to $200,000 for a 60-foot-wide lot, was $800,000 to $1.5 million by 2005, Knowles says. As of 2005, he says, there were about 935 year-round residents, and the number was going up.

There are some restrictions. The town's height limits have varied in recent years between 45 and 50 feet—either of which would have precluded several structures built earlier.

(By comparison, Topsail Beach allows a 38-foot maximum height. Surf City has a 48-foot restriction, except for some 60-foot structures allowed under an ordinance covering the marina area.)

Knowles says half the town can't get federal flood insurance because of the lay of the island. Private insurance is very expensive. The north end is being carried away. "They call them 'inlet housing areas' for a reason," he says. He laughs a little when he adds, "Serenity Point, down at the south end of the island, they've got all the sand down there that we used to have."

Still, the beaches are inviting. The town is looking at a 50-year beach renourishment program that would involve pumping up sand from the ocean, increasing the width of the protective dunes, and planting sea oats and grass. It already boasts public-access points to the beach and a new park.

This is a paradise everywhere you look. The idea is to keep it.

Knowles thinks he has a handle on the allure of Topsail, and it's not just that of a beach community. He has lived on Hilton Head and in Myrtle Beach. "One of the things that attracts people here is it's sort of secluded. You don't have the commercial aspect of Myrtle Beach and Wrightsville Beach. It's still an old-timey town. It's a little bit of that out-of-the-wayness."

Knowles already has lived longer in North Topsail than anywhere else. "I didn't have any idea this would be the last place I'd ever live." He laughs. He has no intention of leaving.

Rusty and Mary Brashear moved from suburban Chicago to North Topsail in the summer of 2005, retiring to a new five-bedroom home they helped design. They had been looking for a retirement spot on the East Coast and seen a small ad in the *Wall Street Journal* several years earlier. North Topsail was "incredibly reasonable," Rusty says, adding that it's less so now. They bought property for an investment. The plan was to build on Kiawah Island in South Carolina. But Kiawah became even more pricey, even more exclusive, and it no longer appealed to the couple. They sold their Kiawah property and built on Topsail. In fact, once they moved down, they put their second home on the market, too. Their second home was in France.

Rusty laughs. He has heard since then of "the folly of building on the beach." Neither he nor Mary thinks it much of a folly to build on Topsail. "Only people who don't live here think that," Mary says. "The people who can't imagine why you would build here haven't seen it."

They were drawn to the beauty of the island, the family orientation, and Topsail's relative lack of development. They've built on the beach, still uncrowded. They can see the pier from their beach; it's a 10-minute run for Rusty. "It was the type of place we went to when we were younger and when our kids were younger," Mary says, alluding to Jekyll Island and other Georgia islands. Rusty's story is similar. "The first place I came to was Myrtle Beach—before Myrtle Beach was Myrtle Beach."

The huge houses and the skyrocketing real-estate assessments have taken some of North Topsail's long-timers aback. At a town meeting, Rusty remembers some people wanting the "houses smaller, to turn back the time. But everyone knows the property's going to develop." Moreover, he adds, North Topsail is a town with virtually no businesses; it needs the tax base of the large homes.

Most of the new homes are rental units. The Brashears wish they weren't the only year-round residents on their

Nature takes away and man puts back, especially at North Topsail Beach. Sand is replaced after every major storm.

street. "I really don't want to see any more rental duplexes," Rusty says. "I would love to see single-family development." Indeed, they were more than a little apprehensive when a rental house with eight bedrooms went up next door—a rental house that sleeps 28 people. The renters turned out to be family groups that vacation together. The Brashears have enjoyed meeting new families every few weeks. "It really is nice, and it's the way our family used to vacation," Mary says. As long as the island's owners keep renting to families and not to younger renters wanting party houses, things should be fine, she says.

They are talking on a blustery February day, when their patio furniture has to dig its feet in against the wind. "You assume there's always a chance the whole thing will be blown away," Rusty says. But the couple's house is as sturdy as they come, built to be hurricane resistant with strong walls and

"Dade County" windows designed to take 160-mile-an-hour winds.

"You can live your life in fear," Mary says, "or live every day of your life without fear in a beautiful place."

CHAPTER ELEVEN

Vacations

Only a few thousand people live on Topsail Island year-round—about 3,000, at last estimate. Though the number grows each year, the island remains primarily a summer vacation retreat. Several hundred thousand people visit during the summer months, perhaps 15,000 to 20,000 each week, maybe more than that, according to the area's chamber of commerce. No one has a precise number.

Most are families. Some are fishermen. Many are people who get the island in their blood and return year after year. Children return to Topsail as adults, and the cycle continues. Many families have been visiting for three or four generations.

Their vacation stories are remarkably similar and unwaveringly memorable, yet filled with simple pleasures. Woven together from the 1950s into the 21st century, the stories tell of swimming and fishing, sunrises and sunsets, hurricanes and floods, sunning and skating, miniature golf and ice-cream sodas, dating and gathering with friends.

Together, they make the tapestry of Topsail.

Alan Watson, a history professor at the University of North Carolina at Wilmington, got his love for the Carolina coast at an early age. His family vacationed every summer at Topsail from 1953, when he was 11, to 1960.

There were few people here in the 1950s. The building of a bridge at Surf City had begun to open the island to visitors. Still, Watson says, "there was practically nothing from Surf City to Topsail Beach. I remember my uncle wanted to buy some beer, and Pender was a dry county. He had to drive to Surf City and into Onslow County."

Hurricane Hazel hit in 1954. When Watson's family returned the next summer, Topsail Sound, a favorite swimming place for a young boy, was now off-limits. Filled with debris and even complete houses that had been swept off their foundations, the sound was too dangerous for swimming. At least the family found a cottage to rent. They were fortunate in that, as Hazel had destroyed many of the island's rental properties. Even the cottage next door to theirs, while still standing, had been knocked askew. Walking inside, Watson remembers, made one feel disoriented and queasy.

That was an eventful summer. Watson remembers a historic baseball game he saw at the Breez-way Inn, next to the sound. "I remember watching the All-Star Game in '55, when Stan Musial hit his home run in the 12th inning to win the game. It was very exciting. I think that was the only TV on the island."

Sometime in the mid- to late 1950s, Watson witnessed a drowning in a channel on the inland side of the island.

"There was a man and his child. I don't know if it was a boy or a girl." The child was in trouble in the too-deep water. "The man went in to save his child," Watson says, "and he held the child above his head. He died in the process of saving his child."

Watson ruefully acknowledges he also has firsthand knowledge of real-estate prices back then. "A beachfront lot in Topsail Beach in 1957 could be had for $3,000," he says. "I know because my father had a lot, briefly. He sold it later." Watson laughs. "The family sometimes regrets that he did."

Evelyn Bradshaw remembers vacations with three friends, young mothers all. The first time was in 1961. When her friend Jane Bland Watson mentioned she had a beach house on Topsail, Evelyn's interest was piqued. It wasn't much at all, Jane cautioned her. It was really more of a fishing shack than a cottage. There was electricity but no running water. Evelyn was hardly dissuaded. "You have a beach house!"

They came up for a weekend that first time, the four women, to play bridge. They brought their small children. "We had to park on the road and haul all our stuff down to the sound side to this shack," Bradshaw recalls. The house had only one big room, with curtains for privacy. The visitors slept on metal cots.

Bathing might have been difficult without running water, but Hurricane Hazel had deposited, of all things, a bathtub. "We filled it up in the morning with pump water," Bradshaw says, "and it was heated by the sun all day." Each of the children took a bath at the end of the day. The next morning, the process was repeated.

At night while the children slept, the moms played cards and talked. That was her introduction to Topsail, Bradshaw says.

The cottage was between Topsail Beach and Surf City. It

Evelyn Bradshaw, with husband Hoyt, has spent much of her life on Topsail. Her first visits were as one of four mothers staying in a friend's bare-bones fishing shack. Fortunately, there was a bathtub dropped off by a hurricane. "We filled it up in the morning with pump water, and it was heated by the sun all day," she says. The children bathed at night. The next day, the process was repeated.

seemed they had the island virtually to themselves. "Once we got out in the water, we took our clothes off," Bradshaw remembers. They tied the clothes to inner tubes, confident no one was around.

Change came. Sometime in the 1970s, Topsail began to be built up. "People discovered it. It was a cheap place to buy a piece of property."

Year after year, the Bradshaws came back with the children. "We played all week, then on Friday night would take them to town. Skating rink and the Putt-Putt—that was the entertainment. Everybody skated. The rest of the week, they learned how to crab and they swam."

Bradshaw and her husband, Hoyt, eventually moved to the island, settling not far from that original beach shack. Evelyn, one of the island's leading citizens, was instrumental in developing the island's museum. The couple stayed more than two decades but moved off Topsail in 2005, as their advancing years made dealing with storms more difficult. They moved only across the sound to the mainland and remain tied to Topsail by their heartstrings.

So does the next generation. Though they live elsewhere, Bradshaw says, "my children still think of this as home."

Jennifer Cameron Stewart, a third-generation Topsailian born in 1978, has a different perspective of the island but the same love. She spent every summer on Topsail as a child. She lives and works in Raleigh but visits frequently.

Her family has owned a home on Topsail Sound since 1952. Her grandfather Bill Stewart, Sr., bought the home when it was one of about 10 cottages in what would become Topsail Beach. Her father had been diagnosed with polio. The doctor suggested he spend the summer recovering in a humid area, and his mother found Topsail for the family.

Bill Jr. and his family, including his sister Beth, continued spending summers on Topsail. Once recovered, Bill Jr. worked summers for Bush's Marina. "It should also be noted," Jen says of her dad, "that the man spent his teenage years terrorizing the neighbors and skiing on my grandmother's barstools." He and his friends would leave Jeep tracks on the beach to lure unsuspecting beachgoers in their cars, then show up to pull them out of the sand and make a few bucks. The money went to gas up the boats. One of those friends once ran his boat full speed into a pier, shearing the top off. The friend lived because he ducked.

Jen, her sister Kellie, and their two cousins—born between

1972 and 1981—all spent summers on the island working in the restaurants at the Breezeway and the Beach Shop. "The Sound Pier, in its heyday, was where all the kids would walk for candy treats and ice cream. The Putt-Putt is where my generation went to meet the vacationers and flirt, and across the street was the Jif-Freeze with ice cream. The Jif-Freeze building now holds Topsail Island Seafood, which is owned by two brothers that were raised on Topsail and were always up to something, but the best of guys to my sister and me."

Those are hardly her only memories of summers in Topsail Beach. She rattles off the names of lifelong friends made on the island. "I've witnessed two piers falling in—the Sound Pier and our own," she adds.

Bill Jr., Beth, and their spouses now own the home. The family recently rekindled a neighbor's old event. Every year, they used to gather next door for "Harvey's Fourth of July Bash." In 2005, more than a decade after Harvey Gordon's death, they brought back the get-together. "We have a gazebo on our pier that Harvey built," Jen says, "and one of the windows is a complete circle rather than a semicircle. Harvey built the full circle as 'Michael B's window,' a tribute to his grandson that is there to this day." Today, that grandson is a man. "The window serves more as a tribute to Harvey now."

The generations continue on Topsail. Jen's sister Kellie has a daughter, Hope, born in 2001. "As a true fourth-generation 'Top-sul-ite,' she loves 'her' beach house."

Not everything is the same, however. Due to soaring house prices since the turn of the 21st century, many neighbors they knew as children are selling.

Not the Stewarts. "If you don't get a little salt in your soul as often as possible," Jen says, "it's just not living."

CHAPTER TWELVE

The Collapse

*D*uring *the 1970s and 1980s, the Fourth of July always meant fireworks on the Topsail Sound Pier in Topsail Beach.* Hundreds would surge onto the large T-shaped pier near the southern end of the island to ooh and aah as colorful displays exploded above the sound. The event was a summer highlight on the island. Many who were not on the pier gathered where they could see the fireworks anyway.

The annual spectacular came to a crashing end in 1987, though, the victim of an accident that was startling, nearly tragic, and then, finally, sobering. It began, says Topsail Beach police chief Rickey Smith, when one of the fireworks shot from the beach went awry. The missile headed not out over the water but over the pier. Though it was high enough not to endanger the 300 who were gathered, momentary panic ensued anyway.

"The people all ran to one side of the pier, everyone," Smith says. The quick shift of weight was more than the pier could handle. "It popped one of the pylons."

With a support broken, a 20-foot portion of the pier simply gave way. The collapsed section was now in the shape of a V. Some 30 people went sliding and falling into the sound. The image may seem funny in hindsight, many of the island's notables flailing about in the water below, including the mayor, who was the pier's owner. It was anything but comical. The collapse began a nightmarish chain of events. Electrical wires that ran current to the pier's lights snapped and dangled in the water. Some of the victims were surely injured. Perhaps some had drowned or been electrocuted. Meanwhile, most of the guests, farther out on the pier, were now cut off from the mainland.

Topsail Beach police found they were overwhelmed. Smith called in police and ambulances from every available entity, including Surf City, Pender County, Onslow County, New Hanover County, the North Carolina Highway Patrol, and even the North Carolina Wildlife Resources Commission and the North Carolina Marine Fisheries Commission. A swarm of emergency vehicles descended on Topsail Beach.

Help came by water as well. Small boats were volunteering to pick up people. Smith called in the Coast Guard to evacuate those stranded on the remaining part of the pier. Rescue workers went to work dealing with the victims. Some had suffered broken bones. Others had electrical burns. The pier's owner, Mayor Kip Oppegaard, rushed to help the rescue workers. But Oppegaard was overcome by chest pains and had to be hospitalized himself.

The chaos was about to get worse. A wire-service reporter had been on the pier and called in the news, Smith says. But

A large crowd and a sudden shift of weight led to the collapse of the Topsail Sound Pier during a Fourth of July fireworks display in 1987. In this newspaper picture, boaters look at the damage the following day. There were no deaths but a number of injuries from the collapse, which signaled the end of fireworks at the Topsail Beach pier. Fireworks have since resum)ed in Surf City.
(*Wilmington Morning Star*)

details became garbled between the call and broadcast reports on radio and TV. What emerged was a small-town *War of the Worlds* scenario. Listeners were told not that the Topsail Sound Pier had given way but that one of the tall ocean piers had. They heard not that 30 people had fallen into the sound but that hundreds had plummeted into the ocean, Smith says. Many frightened listeners headed to the tiny beach town to check on loved ones.

Soon, worried mainlanders were overwhelming the island. The roads of the small beach town, narrow in width and few in number, could not handle the traffic. Smith and other officials gave serious consideration to declaring a disaster, as they would for a hurricane. Instead, the decision was made to set up barricades and ban any traffic other than emergency vehicles.

An 18-year-old woman would tell a Wilmington newspaper, "There was screaming, yelling and people floundering in the water. Some people jumped in to save the people that were floundering." She was rescued by a shrimp boat, as were many others. Because the collapsed V was not entirely submerged, some were able to walk to the other side of the pier. Some used a rope to travel across the V.

A potentially more frightful problem hung over the night. "We didn't know who was on the pier and who wasn't, and we couldn't get an answer," Smith says. In other words, were there bodies still in the sound? The presence of a nearby inlet that could take them out to sea exacerbated the situation. A full answer might not be available for days. "We had Coast Guard helicopters come in with searchlights," the chief says. They hovered above the sound that night, looking for bodies. Fortunately, none were found, and no missing persons would be reported in the days ahead. "It took us all night to clean up the scene. It was a mess for a good while."

The pier collapse proved to be one of the biggest single news events in the island's history, rivaling the visits of Hurricanes Bertha and Fran nine years later. Television and newspaper reporters swarmed the pier. National publications and networks reported the collapse. A banner headline ran across the top of page 1 of Wilmington's newspaper the next morning, and the morning after that as well. The story remained front-page news for most of the week.

There were no deaths. But 16 people had been injured. Of those, 11 were taken to Wilmington hospitals. A newspaper article five days later reported two remained there, including Oppegaard. One Pennsylvania woman had fractured her ankle so badly the bone broke the skin, but still she swam for shore, holding her four-year-old son aloft for several minutes until someone jumped in to help. A friend said he and the woman had joked minutes earlier about the pier's apparent unsteadiness. "She said, 'This thing sways a little bit, doesn't it?' " the man told the *Wilmington Morning Star*. "I said something like, 'Oh, they all do.' . . . Then, 15 minutes later, just all of a sudden, flop. It just collapsed. The joke was on us."

· It was a 65-year-old woman, however, who fared worst. Sustaining both a broken left shoulder and electrical burns, she needed six hours of surgery at a hospital in Sanford to receive a prosthetic ball joint for her shoulder and skin grafts on a leg. Months of recuperation would follow. Her daughter, whose hands were burned by live wires brushing against her wet skin, described the sensation to the *Morning Star* as akin to a "jackhammer tearing up a slab walkway. . . . I just kept screaming over and over for someone to turn it off. When the lights went off, that pain stopped. We were just kind of paralyzed then. I don't know how much longer we could have lived with that current going through us."

The town of Topsail Beach conducted an investigation. The town manager said the possible causes could be narrowed to three—weakened pilings, overcrowding, and "an act of nature." A town ordinance required Oppegaard to keep the pier in repair. Though piers were not regularly inspected, there was no indication he had not been complying.

Civil lawsuits were filed against the mayor. Smith also charged Oppegaard, once he was out of the hospital, with holding a fireworks display without a permit, a misdemeanor. The mayor was convicted after pleading no contest but received a "prayer for judgment continued," which meant no penalty was imposed. "I hadn't been police chief for six months when I had to charge him," Smith says. Some thought the chief had gone too far and that Oppegaard should fire him. The mayor, who had responded bravely at the scene, took the high road again. "His response," Smith says, "was, 'No, he had to do that. It's his job.' I had a great deal of respect for him for saying that." Others did, too, for the way Oppegaard had handled the tragedy.

Though storms have since done it in, the Topsail Sound Pier was repaired and reopened after the 1987 incident. But Oppegaard never staged another display. He had several requests the year following the collapse to resume the popular event. But fireworks now were required to be handled by an expert, and Oppegaard could find none. The mayor was philosophic, however, quoting a popular TV commercial in an interview with the *Morning Star*. "I might flick my Bic," he said, "but that's about the only thing I can do this year."

Fireworks would return to Topsail one day—but up the island in Surf City, and not until years later.

CHAPTER THIRTEEN

Cottages

*T*he story of Topsail can be see in its hous-
*es, from 1950s cottages to 21st-century duplexes
and mansions.* Start on tiny Shore Drive in
Surf City, just a few hundred feet from the
ocean, and head south. The road is narrow
and demands a casual pace. Beachgoers cross
the street. Children play. Small cottages line
the road, their chain broken here and there
by new, larger homes.

There is time to look.

On this part of Topsail Island, one of the
first developed, most are one-story homes,
though they are elevated to two-story height
by pilings, mandatory on this hurricane-vul-
nerable spit of land. Weathered gray decking
is the rule, too—a standard, a given, seemingly as essential to a Topsail home as roofing.
Towels and bathing suits are draped over the
railings.

There is something more. Most homes have names. Not family names, though there are those, too. House names.

Tranquility By the Sea. Peace by the Sea. No Regrets. Stargazer.

The Reason Why.

Some are funny or whimsical, some a play on words. Thought went into all the names—more thought, it sometimes seems, than went into paint color.

The names speak of good times or suggest a sense of humor. They speak of lifelong dreams reached, of retirement in a blissful place, of the reasons why people are here.

They speak of what is important.

Beach Beauty, The Oceanic, A God Thing, Tak-It-Easy, Misty Sea, Wave to God.

Trivial Pursuit, Land 'N' Strip, Snail's Pace.

Seaclusion.

Continuing on Shore Drive, a driver caught up in the name game unconsciously begins to slow even more.

The names, coming one after another, begin to give a feel of the island. They tell the story of what Topsail means.

Bout Time, Bunnie's Hutch, Our Mint Julep, Nothin Fancy, Sea Magic, Beach Mountain, Beach Rover, Journey's End, Seaside Serenity.

Sand Doodles, Shimmery Waters, Cuckoo's Nest, Sea Urchin II, Life Saver, A Beach Place.

Seas the Day.

Some signs are little more than painted plywood. Most are more elaborate, though, whether homemade or professionally crafted. They are colorful, sometimes enhanced with paintings or other artistry. They catch the eye.

Surf's Up, Salty Dawgs, Dubs & Scrubs, Teacher's Pet.

Topsail Terry.

Pink Palace of Topsail.

Permanent homes began showing up on Topsail in the late 1940s and 1950s. At first, they were little more than glorified shacks built by fishermen or vacationers or, just as likely, instant real-estate agents. Year-rounders then joined them. Topsail cottages over time would incorporate what initially had been luxuries: electricity, running water, and, later, air conditioning.

In the early days, cottages were built at ground level, usually one story, often on a concrete slab. But ground level at Topsail has a nasty habit of turning into below-water level, thanks to hurricanes and flooding. New local governments began taking zoning power, and Topsail homes from then on were elevated. They might not withstand a hurricane, but if they did, they were likely to be safe from the ensuing floodwaters. Soon, new homes could no longer be built on the beach either. They needed to be on the inland side of protective sand dunes.

Shore Drive stops here, then takes an abrupt left turn onto the island's main north-south road. The island now is too narrow for more than one through road, and so Shore joins N.C. 50.

Nearly all the homes are named on Shore Drive and, as it is called a few miles south in Topsail Beach, Anderson Boulevard. The colorful signs are as ubiquitous here as house numbers.

The names on the Topsail Sound side are taken from life stages, dreams, previous homes, even Jimmy Buffet music.

Hog Heaven, Fun N Sun, Empty Nest II, Sea Scape.

Parrothead Quarters.

Island Crib, Sunny Beaches, Windswept, C Shell, The Rusty Pelican, South Wind.

Mid Summer Beach Dream.

License to Chill.

Topsail Island cottages range from half-century-old homes built on concrete slabs to large, modern duplexes. A small part of the allure surely lies in the colorful names homeowners give them, much as boat owners bestow names upon their craft. Many vacationers return to the same cottage year after year, generation after generation.

Ex-Conns, School's Out, Bikini Bottom, Stow-Away.
Mother Ocean.
Beach Nutz, Sandy Pawse, Sail Into the Mystic, The 5th Chip, Sea N Sound, Time Out, The Yellow Beach House, The Sandcastle, Breath of Heaven, Beach's Beacon, Jolly Mon, Beach Music.
A Delay in Time.
Breakaway, The Scotch Bonnet, Shore Enough, Barefootin' at the Beach.

There is a subtle difference in the collection of names on the ocean side. Cumulatively, they weave a Topsail tapestry.

The Survivor, Southern Comfort, Palm Trees Resort, C Watch, Surf Song, Full Timeout, Sea Bees, Island Holiday, Pelican Palace, Dream Catcher, Whale Song, Oceancrest, Gem.
Fins to the Right.

Gull Friends.

Fins to the Right.

Yes, two *Fins to the Rights*, just two houses from one another. One wonders who named theirs first.

Ten Forward, Heaven Sent, The Lazy Gator, La Danse des Dauphins, 3 by the C, Next 2, Sea Wind, Twin Landings, Sand Castles, Cashelmara, Happy Ours, Rise & Shine, Pelican's Bill, Montana Café, Coo's Next, Dolphin Watch, Sea & Me, Sundance, Manana.

Topsail Turvey, Dolphin Den, Serendipity, Shell Seekers, Time in a Bottle, Sea Hawk, Endless Summer, Plan B, Topsider Happiness, Roll Tide, Escape Hatch, Beachcomber, Seashells and Shark Teeth, En the Right Place.

Ocean Commotion, Sea Haven, Longest, Sea Section, On the Beach, C Oats, Crabby Shack, Brother Joe's, Old Yeller, Summer Daze, Kickin' Back, Mahi-Mahi, The Beach Nuts, Loggerhead, Sweet T, Legal Pad, Lazy Daze, Beach Haven.

Looney Dunes, Tee Time.

A Shore Thing.

Squirrelly Banana, Treasure, The Tortuga, La Pescada, Gritty Britches, Pura Vida, Footprints in the Sand, Holiday Haven.

Turn around at Surf City's center, then head toward North Topsail Beach on the main road. The names are different enough to warrant notice.

Farmer's Tan, C-Oats.

Parrot-ise.

From Coats to Coast.

Turtle Dunes, Reflections, Beach Tracks, Surf's Up, Island Gamble.

Jewel of the Isle.

In North Topsail, many homes are newer, bigger, pricier. So are many signs. Homemade signs give way more frequently to large, professionally crafted ones, probably installed by a builder or developer or added by a real-estate agent renting the property.

Sea Monkey Bungalow, On the ½ Shell, Sea Ponies, Splash Landing, Anita Beach, The Sand Hassle, Weedidit, Absolut Bliss, Ryan's Hope, Maine Barracks.

Almost Heaven, Dream Weaver, Just Chill'n.

Nextasea.

Footloose, Fancy Free.

Up on the Roof.

Gone Coastal.

God's Grace, Flamingo Crossing.

Infini-Sea.

Five Buoys, Dolphin Watch.

Naming cottages is a quaint island tradition that seems likely to endure even as Topsail homes become larger and more expensive. What is special to people is worth naming.

Live on the island near the water, in other words, and you may know what it's like to be Nextasea, living your Mid Summer Beach Dream.

Or perhaps at last you will know The Reason Why.

CHAPTER FOURTEEN

Photographs

Vacationers *rarely come to Topsail with-out a camera.* Opportunity presents itself again and again. There is the natural beauty of pristine beaches, sand dunes draped with sea oats, ocean sunrises, sound-side sunsets, sea gulls and sandpipers, even dolphins in the surf. And there are unique structures: the swing bridge leading onto the island, long fishing piers, steadfast concrete towers from the missile program. There are fireworks for the Fourth of July, a flotilla of lighted boats in late November, and festivals in between. There are tourists, fishermen, boaters, swimmers, beach walkers, shoppers, surfers.

And there are families who come back year after year, decade after decade, generation after generation. Their histories are built summer by summer.

Sitting in her living room in Richmond,

Virginia, Kris Chapin goes through boxes of family photographs. She's visited Topsail nearly every summer for more than three decades, first as a child and then as an adult—some years several times a summer—and now she has more Topsail photos than can be counted, it seems, or placed in albums.

And she has more memories than photographs.

"This is my sister Beth and me—and my dad," Chapin says, pulling out pictures from 1974, their first summer on the island. The sisters and their late father, Stan Joynes, Jr., are standing in the surf. There's a second picture of the girls standing in back of their cottage, holding fishing rods, a small dock extending into Topsail Sound behind them. There's a third of them on the dock.

Topsail was the summer place for dad Stan, mom Betty, and two of their three daughters, Beth and Kris. Stan III and Ginger were older and didn't make the trips on a regular basis. But Betty's sister Ginny and her grandson Chris were there.

Kris Chapin especially remembers her dad at Topsail. "He used to go out there late, always by himself, and float or body-surf," she says. She laughs. "That was shark feeding time, which we didn't know at the time."

Chapin pulls out a 1976 photograph of her sister and herself, both noticeably taller those two years later. Also pictured are cousins Chris and Quinn, the latter the granddaughter of Thelma and Sam Raspberry, the cottage owners. She guesses the photograph was taken by her mom or dad. "They didn't take pictures very often. I guess that's why I became a photographer."

The Rasberrys' Topsail Beach cottage—which the Joyneses occupied until moving next door in 1982—was among the island's early ones. "Sonny Jenkins helped Sam build that house." Jenkins is a long-timer on the island, famed now for running the skating rink with his wife, Doris, and for building exquisite birdhouses. The cottage was a small one-story built on the ground. That was before Hurricane Hazel hit in 1954. It was bare bones, as virtually all Topsail cottages were, Chapin remembers. "No TV, no phone, having to remember to wear flip-flops before you opened the refrigerator so you wouldn't get shocked."

The big outing was to the Breezeway for dinner. "While we were waiting for food, Chris and I would go outside and play on the sea wall, chasing the little black crabs" that lived in the piles of shells. Another night, they might go for ice cream at the old Jif-Freeze. Nearby was Cherry's, painted pink, now Skully's Pub and Grub. She's got the photographic documentation that Cherry's was indeed pink. The Putt-Putt used to be yellow.

One of the island hot spots was the skating rink, run by the Jenkinses atop the town post office. "We didn't do much skating as kids, except in the street. We didn't do too much that cost money," Chapin says. "We played a lot of cards, swam all day, and hunted for sharks' teeth. Beth had the best eye for finding them, and still does."

Kris and her husband, Neal, have taken their own children to the skating rink, and, yes, there are photographs. The skating rink is a true throwback, virtually unchanged. "It sounds awful, the speakers are shot," she says of the music, laughing. "The railings are metal and probably not very safe, but that's part of the charm of it." It's just as it was, still un-air-conditioned and still popular. "When we went in July, probably 30 people or more were there. It's hot and sweaty, but there's a box fan for every single window, and there are 15 or 20 windows." In August, crowds are smaller.

So much else has changed on Topsail Island, though, whether altered by man or simply reclaimed by nature.

Chapin pulls out a 1983 photograph of the three-level Sea

Vista Motel, taken postcard-like from the beach. A storm later would wipe out the first floor. Another old picture shows the one-story Gift Basket. A second floor would be added later. Chapin sifts through pictures to a pack from 1984. A picture taken from in front of the Sea Vista shows homes that are no longer there. Here's a black-and-white of the Sea Vista, looking down Ocean Boulevard. The photograph seems even more ancient among colored prints.

Here are several of the old Topsail Sound Pier, shot from the backyard of the Chapins' rental cottage in 1984. The pier, which held a market late in its life, is now gone. She wasn't there but remembers the Fourth of July celebration when part of the pier gave way.

A 1985 picture shows the missing missile tower. All eight tracking towers from the government's top-secret missile program still stand save this one near the northern end of the island. In the picture, the dilapidated tower is abandoned and covered in graffiti. It had wider window openings than most of the other towers.

Here are Joynes and Chapin pictures of family from 1990, small cottages from 1983, beach damage from 1984, a scenic dune from 1984, sunsets in the sound from 1984, and family from the dock out back of the cottage in 1991.

Chapin has an eye for scenery.

The Topsail Sound Pier was wiped out by a storm, but the remaining pilings stand sentinel in the fading light of a 2000 sunset. Sunrises over the Atlantic Ocean are striking in 2003 photographs. Blow them up and each could be an art print. She has boxes full of them.

A large expanse of sand—Serenity Point at the south end of the island, facing west—highlights a photograph from 2003. Likewise, a startlingly wide expanse of beach dominates a 1991 photo. The beauty and size of the beach at Serenity

Point are difficult to comprehend. Chapin laughs. "People see pictures like that and say, '*Where* is that?' " She laughs. "Not tellin'. I'm not telling."

There is beauty, but there is also devastation.

An August 1996 picture shows bulldozers on the ocean beach. Hurricane Bertha has hit, ravaging the island. The beach and dunes are in the process of being re-created by the bulldozers. No one knew Hurricane Fran would be along soon to make the work futile.

A July 1997 photo shows a Topsail house on the far side of the Intracoastal Waterway. A hurricane the year before had simply moved it far off the island. In the picture, the house remains in the water, nearly having reached the far shore of a marsh. Chapin's zoom lens has brought it within range. A huge expanse of water takes up the picture's foreground—water that the house traversed. A channel marker sits in front of the house. This was the handiwork of either Bertha or Fran. "Bertha gets overlooked. Bertha did some serious damage, too."

Hurricanes are always a story. In August 1995, police drove up and down the streets recommending voluntary evacuation for Hurricane Felix. Kris, three months pregnant with Travis, left with family members. Meanwhile, her older sister and brother-in-law stayed. "The hurricane never came close. It didn't even stir up the surf," Kris laments. "Ginger and Barry had beautiful weather for their remaining five days. Pregnancy must do something to you. I still can't believe I left voluntarily *five* days before we had to!"

Family pictures bring smiles, sometimes outright laughs.

Two photographs from 2003 show their sons fishing on the dock with Neal's father. "I believe that was shortly before Grandpa accidentally threw Colton's brand-new fishing rod into the sound. Boy, did he feel bad about that. He quickly dug out his wallet and bought Colton a new one."

The Chapin boys—Travis, nine years old; Christian, one; and Colton, 13—fish and play in Topsail Sound in this 2005 photograph. Behind them is a pier to which channel dredgers are docked. (Kris Chapin)

A shot from 1991 reminds her how the family assured a visitor in the picture that no one ever fell off the sea wall into the sound. Within 10 minutes, the visitor's son did.

Here's the inside of the house in August 1984. "That couch didn't last through the next storm. It went out with Fran." A 1991 picture shows a large brown stuffed chair worth a laugh these years later. "That's a lovely chair, isn't it? You never know how ugly something is until you take a picture of it." Chapin pauses. "But we still loved the house." A 1998 photo shows the house redone. Since remodeling, they love it more.

Chapin guesses she has taken 500 rolls of film at Topsail, each with two or three dozen photographs. Now all she has to do is put them in about 50 albums and she'll be set.

She comes across dozens upon dozens of pictures from 1993. It was a mother-lode year. Her husband, Neal, was overseas with the Marines. Chapin recorded virtually every movement of their firstborn son, Colton, who was not yet one year old. "I used 14 rolls of film on those two weeks." In this one, she is holding her young son's hand on the beach. "Colton was learning to walk," she says. "He started walking at the beach."

A striking 1993 sunset over Topsail Sound will momentarily slow anyone quickly perusing the photographs. The sky is blue-gray with clouds. The sun, moments from plunging into the sound, is sending a brilliant orange beam across the water to the foreground.

Color abounds. Next is one of the surf, only it's blue-green in color, as if it's a tropical sea somewhere. "There's not a filter on my camera or anything. That looks like the Caribbean."

Sometimes, family and scenery combine. In a memorable photograph from 1993, young Colton is sitting on the sand with a bucket, looking at a shell. A shrimp boat moves in the background. "I blew that one up, enlarged it, because I liked it so much."

Here are Neal and Colton on the beach in 1994, Neal home from overseas. The Topsail sand appears darker and coarser. "Weird. The sand looks really different certain years," Kris says. There were more crushed shells that summer.

Like their mom, the Chapin children have grown to love summers on the island. "Travis wants to move there. He's my laid-back, introspective kid." The boys have grown older. On their several trips a summer to Topsail, Neal Chapin fishes with Colton and Travis, usually off the Jolly Roger Pier. Kris often walks the beach with their youngest son, Christian.

As she goes through her pictures, she finds one of her favorites, from 1994. It reminds her that the house has two very large showers but no bathtub for the young ones. Two-year-old Colton sits in a large cooler. Yes, a cooler, and he is holding a hose. "That's a rite of passage, to take a bath in the Coleman cooler at the beach," Chapin says with a nostalgic laugh. "I wish I had pictures of the others."

Cumulatively, the charm of Topsail comes through in the photographs and the stories of the Chapins and thousands upon thousands of visitors to the island over the past half-century.

The allure of Topsail, Chapin says, is "that it's stuck back in the '50s. There are big open spaces where there could be houses but there aren't. People aren't flying around. It's so clean. When I go to Virginia Beach, I don't go on the beach. It feels dirty; there are cigarette butts everywhere. But Topsail, if there's trash, you pick it up." There's more. "People talking to you. There's a bond by sharing the same place. . . . It's a different kind of place."

A picture may be worth a thousand words.

Even so, Topsail is worth a thousand pictures.

CHAPTER FIFTEEN

The Law . . .
and the Bear

S*mall-town policing has a charm that can belie its seriousness of purpose.* It may look like Sheriff Andy and Deputy Barney, but police chiefs in Topsail Island's three small towns will tell you it's a job to be taken seriously.

Still, you can't help thinking . . .

Walk into the office of Michael Halstead, the Surf City chief of police since 1999, and his first words, after the introductions, are not about police work. They are about writing. "I'm writing a crime novel about serial killings on an island," the chief says, smiling. "But I named it Sun City. And the mayor's a bad guy." It is, he is quick to say, completely fictional.

If you want violent crime on Topsail Island, you have to make it up.

There's been only one homicide in Surf City's history, Halstead says. An intoxicated boyfriend beat a woman's two-year-old child to death in 2002. The horrific crime brought a sentence of life plus 50 years. "We have your typical beach issues, bar fights, car accidents." Fender-benders are common. Not only does Surf City's own traffic come through this middle-of-the-island town, but because of the island's configuration, so does all of Topsail Beach's traffic and much of North Topsail Beach's. There are house fires from time to time. There was more drug trafficking when he took over, Halstead says, but aggressive policing has cut that.

Violent crime is almost nil. Surf City has about 2,000 residents in the winter but swells to perhaps 40,000 or 50,000 in summer, Halstead says. His estimate is higher than most, but then his territory is growing rapidly. Halstead has 13 full-time officers plus four sworn reserves. As Surf City continues expanding onto the mainland, his force may more than double its size by 2010, Halstead guesses.

So is this Mayberry?

"There have been some people who have told me that," Halstead says, laughing. "They have told me I'm Andy Griffith, or Andy Taylor." He considers the question and decides that he and the fictional small-town sheriff do have at least one thing in common. "It is a laid-back town."

Halstead has a "Park and Walk" program. Each officer must make eight introductory visits a day—five to homes and three to businesses. The officers get out of the car, introduce themselves, ask how they can help. There's an "Are You OK?" program, in which the elderly can sign up for daily phone checks. And there's a "Watch Your Car" program, in which you put a sticker on your car and police will pull over the driver if the car is out too late. That's the approach. The police in Surf City make themselves visible to dissuade criminals. They practice community relations.

And the chief works on a murder mystery during his off hours. Halstead may see about getting it published. It's entitled "Murders in the Sand." It's about the fictional Sun City, remember. The real Surf City is quite different.

The chief leans back in his chair. "This is a real nice town," he says.

When a lunch-hour visitor arrives at the North Topsail Beach Police Station, he is greeted with a sign that reads, "Closed for lunch. Will return at 1:00."

North Topsail Beach may be Topsail's boom town, but it's still small-town. "This is basically a family-oriented beach," Chief Danny Salese says. "We've been watching kids grow up over the years, coming back every summer."

Daniel R. Salese III, a graduate of the FBI Academy, has been chief since 1998, six years after he came to the department. He has a force of 11 full-time and six reserve officers. And he bristles at the Mayberry analogy. This is real policing. There are drunk-and-disorderly calls, bar fights, domestic fights, he says, and sometimes more. "Officers have had to draw their guns on people. Yes, we've had felons here. Yes, we've had people wanted for murder [elsewhere] arrested here. If it comes our way, we're ready to deal with it." He and the force take pride in their training and professionalism in combating things people would rather not know about.

"People think it's Mayberry because they're not experiencing it," he says. "One of the reasons they don't is police patrols. We're sweeping it up at night."

Salese's department gets calls for theft and vandalism, often involving construction workers who live in condominiums

153

while working on the myriad new homes. There are fire calls, too, and ambulance calls. This being an island, there are swimmer-in-distress calls. The police also run an all-terrain-vehicle beach patrol and even a water patrol with boats and Jet Skis. And because the town is nearly half the length of the island, officers must be stationed at several spots for quick response.

Still, the department uses a small-town approach. "We help you out," Salese explains. "We still help change tires. We'll be down there jump-starting cars, unlocking car doors." North Topsail police check on the elderly and volunteer information to tourists.

And when homeowners leaving in the fall forget to turn off the water or even to close a window, they call the police. "We find a lot of open doors, open windows. We've got officers who climb second-story windows to close them," Salese says with a smile. "People are shocked we'll help them."

If there is a Sheriff Andy Taylor here, it is most likely Rickey Smith of Topsail Beach, the small, old-fashioned town that comprises the southern stretch of the island.

"Mayberry, exactly," says Smith, the island's veteran chief, having come to the department in 1983 and become its chief in 1987. He laughs at the pervasiveness of the theme. "People are all the time yelling at me, have I given this officer his bullet yet?"

Topsail Beach has seven full-time officers—including two lieutenants and four patrolmen—and Smith is proud of their professionalism. He has seven sworn reserves. And yes, all his officers have more than one bullet.

Smith can't escape the Mayberry comparison. Nor does he try to. "I'm so thankful it's like that," he says. "We've managed to stay a small department. The town has kept its attitude of being a small retirement-type community. Our crime rate is still one of the lowest crime rates anywhere in the area." In the past decade, he says, there have been fewer than 50 break-ins. That's 50 total. Credit the small population. There are only 1,500 homes, and 1,300 of those are empty come wintertime. There's no bridge to the town either, so there's only one way in and out—the main road to Surf City. That makes policing easier.

When Smith took over, though, his was only a four-man department, and break-ins were a scourge. He put officers in marked patrol cars, increased their daily patrol mileage from 30 to 100, and set one car up near the Surf City line. Police began checking on parked cars and drivers who appeared to be sleeping, once breaking up a group stealing TV sets from a motel by doing so. "We can be aggressive because no one comes down here just to drive and look around in the middle of the night," Smith says. The year before he arrived, the town had 42 burglaries. Within a few years, it was down to 12. Now, it's no more than five a year.

The island setting makes police work a little different than in other small towns. The department runs a boat in the channel behind the island, Smith says. It also has a motorcycle and an all-terrain vehicle to assists beachgoers.

Smith has had one decidedly un-Mayberry-like case. The April 28, 1990, *Wilmington Morning Star* carried a startling banner headline on page 1: "Woman dies in beach burial ritual." A cult had buried several of its members beneath eight to 12 inches of sand as part of a "cleansing ritual." Plastic bags were placed over their heads and snorkel-type tubes in their mouths for breathing, Smith told the paper. An Ohio woman accidentally suffocated.

Smith's town made news again in May 2005. The *Star-News* noted that Topsail Beach and North Topsail Beach were two of four beach towns in southeastern North Carolina that allowed topless bathing by women. More specifically, they had no ordinance against it, as Surf City did. But Smith told the paper there had been few topless bathers, and they had graciously moved to the more secluded southern end. It had never been a problem.

Nonetheless, "Topless Topsail" became big news. In the week following the report, Smith told the paper he fielded about 15 interview requests from news media, one from New Jersey. Property owners called, some upset, wondering if they should sell their vacation homes. Up the island in North Topsail Beach, Chief Salese and others were also fielding irate phone calls, though, as with Topsail Beach, the town had few incidents on its isolated beaches. By midsummer, the issue died out.

The Topsail Beach Police Department is concerned with a different kind of visibility—that of its police officers. Smith continually tells townspeople and vacationers that police are there to help. No issue is too small. "If they're cooking and they need someone to open a jar, call us on down," he says. He means it. "We're never too busy for that." The effort is returned. "We always have somebody cooking dinner for one of our officers on duty and bringing it on over," he says.

Low-key is the manner of choice. In summer, the department sometimes deals with minor issues involving college students who have returned home. Often, the situations are handled unofficially, by talking to parents.

Smith did have one situation he wishes he hadn't. In 1996, islanders who had not evacuated for Hurricane Fran were arrested afterward and charged with violating the town's emergency rule. They weren't happy. Neither was Smith happy about their seeming indifference to the law. They were convicted, but his department asked merely for a promise they would not do it again.

Given the nature of Topsail Beach, it comes as no surprise that Smith once filled in as a building inspector while police chief. At the same time, he was filling in as a zoning officer. Three jobs at once? Actually, it was four. He was filling in as town manager, too. Smith laughs now, but he credits others in the town. Were it not for the community's help, he could not have done them all.

The chief expects to retire by 2008, though only because of heart problems. He can't imagine a better place to work than Topsail Beach. "It's probably as close as you can get to those little communities in the '50s and '60s," Smith says wistfully.

Smith has drawn his gun only once since joining the force. It was for an escapee.

But not an escaped criminal.

A bear.

The call to Chief Smith's home in the wee hours of Wednesday, June 8, 1995, woke him up. The dispatcher said one of his officers had a report of a bear in town. "You-all are playing a game, right?" Smith said. The chief was momentarily annoyed. It was 2:30 in the morning. He didn't need this; he was due up in a few hours for work. The dispatcher answered, "No, sir. I wouldn't call you at this hour to play a game." Smith wasn't convinced. "You sure it was a bear and not just a big dog?" he would ask the officer later.

No bear had ever been at Topsail Beach, as far as he knew. How would it even get there? Deer occasionally find their way onto the island, swimming from a game preserve across the Intracoastal Waterway and maybe across Topsail Sound, too, depending upon where they attempt to cross. Their bodies are sometimes found on the beach. It is a dispiriting sight. "The deer just run into the ocean," Smith says. "They keep running and running, and they get so tired they drown. Their bodies wash up on the shore."

But a bear? Smith got up and went to meet the officer. They would figure this out.

The two patrolled the town separately. It usually takes an hour. They gave Topsail Beach a more thorough going-over, especially in the area where the bear had been reported—toward the south end of town, near the Emma Anderson Memorial Chapel. Nothing. No bear anywhere. As daylight neared, Smith headed home to shower and dress for work.

"And there he was," the chief says. "I actually saw the bear in my neighbor's backyard." Smith was on the main road but could see through the yards to where the bear stood, now in the area between the neighbor's house and his own. The bear, it seemed, had come to meet the chief.

He was hardly to be trifled with. Here was a young-adult male black bear weighing 300 to 400 pounds, experts would say later. The chief called for a state wildlife officer. Meanwhile, the two officers kept an eye on the bear, although what they might do was still a little unclear.

In time, two wildlife officers arrived, and the advice they offered was practical. "They advised me to stay away," Smith says. "We backed away from him." The experts suggested the police try to keep the bear contained in a thicket several blocks long, where he could sleep during the day. Most likely, he would awaken at nightfall and make his way off the island.

The plan seemed to work. Police set up barricades to keep cars off a few blocks of Anderson Boulevard, the main road. The bear was content. What police could not see was trouble beginning on the other side of the thicket—not from the bear but from vacationers. Word had gotten around. Now, a crowd of onlookers was trying to spook the bear. They yelled at him. They threw sticks and pebbles and such into the thicket.

The Law . . . and the Bear

Topsail Island's most frightening visitor since Blackbeard may
have been the black bear that arrived for two days in June 1995.
Police and wildlife officers planned to keep the stray bear in a
wooded area, hoping he would return to the mainland that evening.
But curious vacationers startled him, which drove him out to the
beach. Here, the bear gets his first glimpse of the Atlantic Ocean and
beachgoers. Moments later, the beachgoers got their first glimpse of
the bear—and quickly fled. (Chief Rickey F. Smith)

Smith heard the commotion and hurried to see what it was.
He came around the corner of a utility shed.

So did the bear.

Smith had thought he knew where the intruder was. He
had miscalculated. Bear and man were now face to face. Instantly, Smith unholstered his police Glock .45 caliber gun
for the first and only time on the job. "The bear was scared,
and so was I."

The bear began shaking his head. Smith screamed, but not a
scream of fear. Aware of a young child coming up behind him, he
turned and yelled at her mother. The bear, already skittish, took
heed as well, running in the only direction now open to him.

Out over a dune the bear went, onto the beach.

There he stood on the sand, surveying the Atlantic Ocean,

Urged on by Topsail Beach police, the bear departs, heading up and over the dune and past beach cottages. Police would subsequently keep him contained in a wooded thicket—and keep curious humans away—until he made his way up the island and off it at Surf City. (Chief Rickey F. Smith)

seeing a sight he had likely never witnessed. "He must have thought it was the largest river he had ever seen," Smith says.

The chief, who had retrieved his police camera from his car, ran after the bear and began taking pictures. One in particular would become a classic: about 20 people lie unaware on the beach as the bear takes it all in, the Jolly Roger Pier in the background. Smith says now he wishes he had clicked again seconds later. "Right after I took that picture, there was nothing out on that beach." A child in the surf had pointed to the bear. Within seconds, the beach was cleared. The sunbathers either ran into the surf or over the dune.

This could have been the script for an episode of *The Andy Griffith Show*—"Andy and the Bear"—except there was now real danger. What might a startled black bear do? "That scared me because there were so many people," Smith was quoted as saying in the following day's *Morning Star*, alongside two of his pictures. "That was the only time I thought about shooting him because I didn't know what he'd do."

The police had learned they could move the bear by making noise. Smith startled him again, this time up and over the dune and past the oceanfront beach houses—another scene photographed by the chief—and into a half-block of woods. Smith clicked three more pictures, including another surreal scene of the bear crossing Anderson Boulevard. The whole beach excursion—and Smith's eight pictures documenting it—had taken only a few minutes.

Some vacationers got a treat in those moments. "I was lying on the beach when I heard people scrambling," one man told the Wilmington paper. "I looked up and saw this jet-black bear walking down the dunes and some guys walking behind him. He looked almost tame walking down the beach that way." Another visitor said she hadn't seen the bear but would not have been afraid. "In fact, I hope we see it. We were born here and we've been visiting this beach all our lives, but we've never heard of anything like this."

Smith called the wildlife officers back, and now the four men kept tabs on the visitor—and on any onlookers. The bear stayed in the thicket roughly bounded by Barwick and Haywood avenues. Not only Anderson was barricaded, but side roads as well. There was nothing to do but wait. "We had to baby-sit him," Smith says.

Experts later would say bears are relatively common along the North Carolina coast and indeed once were found on Topsail. Blackbeard may or may not have visited the island, but black bears certainly did. Even when Topsail was largely uninhabited, the confrontations were news. The *Wilmington Star* of September 24, 1910, reported, "While on a hunting expedition for marsh hens at Topsail Sound Thursday afternoon, Messrs. W. P. Walton, W. J. Bradshaw and P. A. Marshburn, of this city, observed a large black bear meandering along the beach on the south side. They were in a boat and watched the animal for about 20 minutes. Mr. Walton stated that he had seen four bears wild in the woods during the past few years and the one seen Thursday was the largest of the number. No effort was made to shoot the bear as the huntsmen did not have their 'bear shot' along."

That was 1910, though. This was 1995, and the Topsail Beach bear found himself in an area far too populated with humans. Wildlife officer Lee Willis told the *Morning Star*, "He doesn't want to be there any more than anyone wants him to be. He's very confused. If everyone will just sit back and let him be, he'll get up at night and go back where he was trying to go. He's really just passing through." The visitor may have been ousted from his territory by another male bear.

About nightfall, the bear did start stirring. Just as the wildlife officers predicted, he began his return trip, heading north. The assumption was that the bear would retrace his steps, most likely to the large game preserve on the mainland. At Surf City, he would need only to cross one waterway to get off the island. Eric Peterson, then the town manager, had another idea of the bear's motivation, quipping to the *Morning Star*, "He just kept going up there. We figure he left his boat up there."

The bear was traveling close to the sound side of the island now, not the ocean side, continually moving north. "He went about five or six miles, through people's backyards, working his way up the island," Smith says. At the town line, the Topsail Beach police handed off their escort duty to Surf City police.

Smith, tired from the 18-hour stakeout, returned home. He was, he admitted later, pretty snippy to his wife. She merely asked why the bear was on the beach. "I reckon," the chief responded, "he came for a vacation like everybody else."

The bear eventually disappeared into a wooded area and

apparently went back home. The *Topsail Island Advertiser* reported the bear may have first made a return visit to the beach. He spent the rest of Wednesday in the maritime forest across from the south end of South Shore Drive. That night, the bear apparently strolled up Shore Drive, crossed the vehicle access near the Surf City Pier, checked out the beach, and finally headed for the Intracoastal Waterway. One Surf City resident reported that she found bear tracks near her home when she went outside to walk her dog Thursday morning. She tracked the bear toward the waterway.

In the days ahead, Smith's pictures made the wandering bear a celebrity. The bear-on-the-beach picture was a particular favorite. Half a dozen local newspapers featured it prominently, and untold others used it in some fashion. At least two TV stations did as well. *Wildlife in North Carolina* magazine would print the picture twice, in issues two years apart. Meanwhile, Smith made about 10 copies for officers. That was hardly enough. "We started getting calls every day, 30 to 100, asking to buy the picture," the chief says. Smith gave the rights to the Greater Topsail Area Chamber of Commerce, which still sells the picture as a fund-raiser. A decade after the bear's visit, Smith received a call from a student doing a research paper on wildlife who wanted to include the Topsail bear. The student was in Japan.

The story of the day the bear came to Topsail lives on in many a telling. The late Lewis Orr, whose fishing pier is seen in the background of the beach picture, told it this way in his 2001 interview:

~~~~~~~

THIS IS A TRUE STORY. A lot of people had trouble believing it. But one summer day, normal summer day that people were on the beach—sunny, the surf was calm, good swimming—and the vacationers down here, the mamas, all had their little children out there, playing in the water. All of a sudden, they looked around, one of them looked around behind her and thought she saw a big black bear coming down the sand dune toward the ocean. Well, she blinked her eyes and looked back again, and he was still there, and he was still coming. She screamed. She had two children in the water, and she ran down there, and she never stopped. She grabbed one of them under each arm and took off back to the motel. Well, by that time, other people, their attention had been drawn to what happened there, and they started running also, so there was a mass flight of people.

The bear, we called the wildlife people, and the police got involved. Thank goodness they didn't shoot him. They didn't even tranquilize him that I know of. Maybe the wildlife people did, unbeknownst to me. But he never damaged anybody. That night, he went back into [the] wooded area just north of the pier. And they tracked him for a day or two, and he wandered on down toward Surf City, and that was the last we heard of him. As far as we know, he swam over here from the mainland; we have quite a few bear over there at the wildlife preserve. But we don't know whether he got back or not. But that's the story of the bear, and it was an unbelievable thing.

It was indeed.
And there are the pictures to prove it.

CHAPTER SIXTEEN

Waters

*F*rom early morning to long after the sun sets, from the beginning of the calendar to the end, the waters of Topsail are part of nearly everyone's life on the island.

Soundside Park is a 19-acre grass-and-water gem that greets Topsail visitors just after they've crossed the swing bridge onto the island at Surf City. The park combines recreation and conservation on 11 acres of land and eight of wetlands.

Arresting images of nature abound any time of year at Soundside Park.

On a warm Sunday afternoon in November, a man reading Tom Wolfe sits in a chair he has placed beside a picnic table. A gentle breeze floats in from the ocean, a few hundred yards distant. A couple strolls nearby. Two young girls run by laughing and almost stumbling, their parents in close pursuit. A man halts his conversation to point out the motionless flight of a sea gull on the wind. If only for a moment, the flight is mesmerizing.

Minutes later, the man gestures toward a seasonal phenomenon. This is a good day to be at the park. Boats are emerging from under the swing bridge on their southward journey along the Intracoastal Waterway. This is hardly unusual; boats going through the bridge opening is practically a year-round occurrence. Now, however, there are not just one or two boats but seven. They are sailboats, mostly, sailboats on parade, with what looks like a houseboat in the middle. The seven are headed toward Florida, part of a month-long flotilla of sailboats, motorboats, fishing boats, and houseboats temporarily leaving the colder climes of the North. The snowbirds will be back in March, coming through the swing bridge again on their return trip.

Soundside Park is a picture snapper's paradise. Sailboats. Egrets and ospreys. Rippling waters. Views of the maritime forest. Sea gulls. A mini fishing pier. A boat ramp. The swing bridge. And sunsets. Perhaps especially sunsets. This late-November Sunday, the sun becomes an orange ball as it reaches slowly for the waters of Topsail Sound, as if posing for the camera.

The photographer who cannot secure a striking image at Soundside Park just isn't trying.

It is early one summer morning, and the only Topsail Beach tourists who have arisen are beach walkers. The late-summer sun is already warming, though, and the waters await. Six deepwater divers who have been staying at the Breezeway Motel carry their gear out the dock behind the motel, then onto a boat.

Their early-morning chat is friendly but clipped, like talk among office workers when they first arrive, before the coffee has been put on. The six are customers of a dive shop in Falls Church, Virginia—a good six- or-seven-hour drive from here—who arrived the night before. They have come for the teeth. Not the tiny black shark teeth that wash up on beaches by the millions, souvenirs for beach walkers with the patience to sift through the sand. These are much rarer finds, the teeth of the prehistoric megalodon. One of the divers, Don Becker, begins to talk as the others go about their business. Megalodons, he says, were huge sharks—four times as big as today's great whites—living off the North Carolina coast between 2 million and 20 million years ago.

The spot to which the divers will carry their search is an underwater ledge. "It was found by Captain Tom while looking for good places to spear fish," Becker says. Tom Collins, who runs Spear-It Dive Charters, captains their boat. The ledge is 105 feet below the surface. That's a serious dive, to a depth not to be trifled with. The divers will breathe from tanks filled with Nitrox, which contains 32 percent oxygen, as opposed to the usual 20 percent. The tanks will give them a full 25 minutes underwater, maybe half an hour. They'll need as much time as possible for the slow, cautious descent and then the return to the surface. Come up too quickly and it may be your last dive.

The waters off North Carolina are a feast for a diver's eyes, and not merely because of the sea life. "The coast right here is the Graveyard of the Atlantic," Becker notes. The story is well known in these parts. The turbulent waters, especially off Cape Hatteras to the north, have sunk many a ship. So, too, did pirates centuries ago, and so, too, did German submarines—U-boats—during World War II. Becker has seen many wrecks on dives—boats of all sizes. Bodies, too? No, he's never seen a body. He assumes the sea creatures dispose of them quickly.

Soundside Park is a picture-snapper's paradise even in winter. Throughout the year, sailboats move past the nearby swing bridge. Egrets and ospreys enjoy the waters. Birds flock to the maritime forest. Sea gulls fly overhead. Vacationers use the boat ramp and the mini fishing pier. And at the end of each day, visitors enjoy kaleidoscopic sunsets over the waters.

The divers will be gone most of the day, motoring into Topsail Sound, around the southern tip of the island, and then out into the Atlantic. They'll say no more than that. Their spot, after all, is their spot. Why spoil a good thing?

When they return, it is midafternoon.

The six—Julie Bedford, Doug Vanderbilt, Joe Brocata, Don and Caste Becker, and Joe Gilbert—unload not only their gear but their treasures as well. The haul has been good. They've brought back many teeth from megalodons and even from the earlier regrolosis. Vanderbilt says the rule of thumb is that one inch of tooth translates to 10 feet of body length. Most of the teeth are four or five inches, meaning the massive ancient sharks, then, were 40 to 50 feet long. Gilbert has found a six-inch tooth, the biggest of the day.

The tip-off to finding megalodon teeth, according to Vanderbilt, is whale bones. "They fed on whales," he says. "Wherever you find a whalebone, you look beneath it and you'll usually find their teeth. They lost their teeth when they fed."

As a bonus, they also found a whale eardrum.

For beach lovers Debra Perdue and Jeannette Godwin, the finds offered up by the sea are less dramatic then megalodon teeth and whale eardrums, but no less satisfying to the soul.

The two friends are fishing off the beach behind their homes in Surf City this fall day, their poles set up in the sand, lines running into the surf. The fishing is not going particularly well. They hope for mullet, black drum, speckled trout, and red drum, Perdue says. Also spot and pompano, Godwin adds. "There are times the shrimpers come in too close," she laments. The shrimp boats are supposed to stay a mile out to sea. "But at 5 A.M., when we're up, they scoop up all our fish."

Perdue says her husband's done better. "He fishes a lot offshore for kings and dolphin. He has had a good year." Dolphin, really? Yes, she says. He goes 15 to 30 miles offshore.

The women are beach walkers, too, scouring the sands for shells and "beach glass" or "sea glass" polished smooth by the waters. As regards these treasures, every day is a good one. Their finds often end up in sea crafts. Perdue has even crafted a patio out back of her home.

The two women and their husbands moved to the island in the mid-1990s. "I've been coming down here since I was a child," Godwin says, "because my daddy loved to fish."

Ann Debnam, who has lived on the island since the mid-1980s and visited before that, walks up. Thirty years ago, she says, it was so quiet. Now, even on a fall day like this, there are people. "This weekend, there were more people down here than used to be here on the Fourth of July weekend." She laughs. "This used to be the poor people's beach." It is getting harder and harder for any but the wealthy to buy on Topsail.

But much of the island's allure remains unchanged. "It's just a family beach," Godwin says. "The friendly atmosphere. It's low-key."

Their husbands go out and fish. They all have dinner. Perdue explains the logistics. "She'll cook dinner one day, I'll cook the next day, someone else will cook the third day." The women are retired but very active. "You walk out every day to see what's going on," Perdue says.

There's always something. "Did you see the porpoises out there this morning?" Debnam suddenly asks the other two. "I saw at least six." The porpoises travel up the coastline, following one another, leaping gracefully into the air, going underwater, and then emerging to repeat the motion. Together, they form a water ballet.

Nature is always at work on Topsail. "Ophelia chopped our dunes in half," Godwin says, motioning to where restoration work is under way.

Debnam motions to the other side of their small group. "Right there, a sea turtle came up and laid eggs, and we got to see it. We called the Turtle Hospital, and they were here right away to block off the area." Perdue agrees. "In two minutes, they were here."

Perdue remembers a recent deer.

Godwin remembers an unusual sight once commonplace. "In 1995, when all the maritime forest was thick, when we were looking for a place to build, we saw raccoons hanging from a tree." They were countless. Everywhere, raccoons were hanging by their tails from tree branches. "Then when the building started, we saw raccoons lying by the road."

For a father and son, the waters of Topsail offer up waves.

Frank and Quinn Blake go surfing whenever there are waves. They would surf 365 days a year if they could, father Frank says. Even now, they come close—"two, three, four times a week," he says.

There are always surfers on Topsail. The island offers good waves, and not just at the appropriately named Surf City. "I've surfed all over the East Coast, and Waikiki, Hawaii," Frank says. Topsail is one of the best spots. The water is warm, and the shape of the waves is often good. "Lined-up peaks, like that wave over there," he says, gesturing off the beach, "only higher."

Beachgoers may prefer smooth water, but surfers don't. "You need to have something to stir the waves," Frank says. In the summer and fall, it can be tropical storms and even hurricanes. They leave the water stirred for days or even longer. In the winter, nor'easters do the trick. "A lot of guys come up from Wrightsville Beach when it's right," he adds. Surfers head onto the island at the same time—and for the same reasons—that many tourists head off.

The Blakes have just come in from some runs this summer morning. Both appear expert, though Quinn claims only that "I'm decent, not great." They'll go back for more in a minute. They often surf for hours.

Frank doesn't volunteer to anyone about the quality of the surfing here, by the way. Enough people know as is. This morning, however, he and Quinn have the waters practically to themselves. Though there are scores of sunbathers and swimmers down the beach, there are fewer than a dozen surfers on this stretch. Turns out it's not yet time for the day's

Surfers walk the beach beneath the Surf City Pier. Topsail's
waters offer swimming, fishing, surfing, kayaking, boating, and even
deep-sea diving.

best surfing. Surfers watch the tide. "You come out here in an
hour," Frank says, "and there'll be 100 people."

There always are.

*Bob Mullen has just been fishing this morning on the Seaview Pier
in North Topsail Beach.* It is Christmas week, and Mullen has
been fishing for trout—not exactly what he would have been
doing in his native Ohio. But the skies are sunny, the wind is
down, and the temperature is approaching 50 degrees.

Mullen and his wife, Janet, moved to the Topsail area in
2003 after vacationing here for 26 years. "For the fishing, and
it's a nice family area," he says. He is a retired physician's assistant and she a nurse anesthetist. They live over the bridge
on the mainland at Sneads Ferry. But they spend countless

hours on the water. Mullen fishes for blues and Spanish mackerel as well as trout. The fishing is excellent, he says.

But the Mullens also do something uniquely Topsailian. "We do a lot of turtle watching," Bob says. In conjunction with a program run by the Turtle Hospital in Topsail Beach, they are assigned a stretch of North Topsail Beach about a mile and a half long. They walk it a couple of times a week. "In the spring, we look for tracks," he says. "We look for eggs." When they find a nest, they contact the hospital staff, which checks the eggs and blocks off the area. Signs alert beachgoers to leave the turtles in peace. Then, in the fall, Mullen says, they watch over the turtles as they head to sea.

They wouldn't be doing that in Ohio either.

Robert Bridges lives here, on Topsail, to fish.

Bridges is a disabled veteran who has been coming to the island since 1999. He used to fish in Wrightsville Beach and Carolina Beach, but he bought a home in Surf City in 2003. "I always liked the beach," he says. "Nice. Peaceful. Can fish anytime I want." He got a deal on the land—and just in time. The property value doubled within two years.

Bridges fishes the surf. "The pier is too expensive," he laments. He usually brings his pole to the beach a couple of times a week. It depends on the tide and the rip current, he says. You can't fish if there's a riptide. Likewise, fish stop running two hours before high tide and two hours after.

This fall day, the whitings are biting, as are spots and black drum. Bridges offers some insight on bait. "A lot of people use sand fleas for whiting. I use shrimp." Maybe it will bring a big catch today. "Hope so. I'm getting tired of eating hush puppies."

Bridges catches a blowfish—not exactly the choice for

someone looking to put dinner on the table. "Want this puffer?" he calls down the beach to Danny Futrell.

Futrell, his own line in the surf, eyes the blowfish. "No," he responds in the clipped conversation of fishermen who know one another. "Uh-uh."

Futrell lives in Wallace, not too long a drive for fishing. He opens up immediately. "I've been coming down here all my life," he says. He guesses he started about 1960. His family would come down two or three times a summer. "Daddy and Granddaddy would fish. We'd play in the ocean."

He sees the island with an old-timer's eyes. "The whole island has been built up so much it's pitiful," he says without rancor so much as resignation. Back in the 1970s, his uncle hesitated about building a home between the roads. There wasn't enough room. Now, four or five condominiums occupy the spot.

Fishermen, once the island's lifeblood, seem to be getting pushed aside. "I used to get a permit and drive up on the beach," Futrell says. He can't do that anymore. He says the decision by island leaders to put in the much-praised pedestrian path along the island's main road in Topsail Beach and Surf City—which vacationers use for walking, talking, and riding bicycles—has come with a price. It has taken the beach fishermen's parking places. "They're thinking more about the tourist dollar and not the fisherman."

He remembers the island used to have six fishing piers. Now, it has three. And a storm last year took away much of the beach. Futrell remembers how big that beach used to be for a boy racing to the ocean. "When I was young, you could run and run and run and your feet was on fire, at low tide, before you could reach the water."

Still, he says, this is the place to be. Spots and mullet have been biting, he says. "I came Saturday and caught a good mess."

174

Night on the beach fills the senses.

The breeze brings the distinctive scent of sea air. The Topsail surf, rough this early-November night, delivers up a heavy mist that not only touches the face but virtually splashes it.

A visitor is immediately enveloped in the experience. Waves thunder in so concussively as to drown out talking. They crash on the beach every six or eight seconds, loudly, powerfully, symphonically. The surf flies. Hands move into pockets. It is chillier down here on the beach.

The moon is only one-quarter full tonight. But it lights, well enough, large tire tracks on the beach. Sand has been brought in again, as it often is following large storms, to replenish the beach. The tracks are evidence of the day's work, at least for now. They will be erased soon.

The waves continue crashing, never losing their beat, never losing their power. Each one throws up more spray.

The only other illumination comes from the Surf City Pier above. Twenty or so lights beam from poles atop the pier, blurring as they emerge from the mist thick as fog. Two dozen fisherman are at work. In five minutes, or 20, most seem scarcely to move.

An artist with a canvas or a camera could have his choice of subjects tonight.

No subject is more striking than the moonlight on the tide—the last subject to catch one's attention, and yet the most compelling. Tonight's light is not enough to fully illumine the beach, but it reflects off the tide magically. All along the beach and far out to sea, the whitecaps catch the moonlight. They glow phosphorescently, as if enhanced by lines of electric lights. It is a magnificent display, a Thomas Kincade painting come to life—were Thomas Kincade paintings continually moving. And 26 miles long.

The waves crash.

It has gotten cooler still. Two visitors pull their sweatshirts tighter and stop to watch.

CHAPTER SEVENTEEN

Turtles

On almost any summer afternoon, a long line of tourists forms in Topsail Beach. They stand outside what looks to be a small one-story home with a large garage.

It is a home, all right, but a home for turtles. The Karen Beasley Sea Turtle Rescue and Rehabilitation Center—most people just know it as "the Turtle Hospital"—is one of the island's main attractions.

On an island that prides itself on maintaining a leisurely pace, it is fitting that the headliners are turtles. The beach may beckon. The fish may be biting. But many families make it a point to come see the turtles. "It's nothing for us to have 300 people lined up outside," says the hospital's director, Jean Beasley. More than 20,000 come each summer to see the Topsail turtles, on view only for limited hours.

Inside what would be called the garage if this were a home are 14 large tanks holding from 75 to 1,100 gallons of water. Most of the tanks are six feet wide or more and perhaps four feet deep; they are reminiscent of above-ground swimming pools. A mural of sea creatures and sea scenes, all in blue, is painted on the walls.

Children ooh and aah, and even parents seem startled at the turtles' size. They are several feet in diameter, some weighing more than a full-sized man. The turtles move by flapping their large flippers. There are repeated *thunks* as they propel themselves into the sides of their tanks. They splash. They create small waves. There is nearly constant motion.

One large turtle per tank is the maximum. "They're not what you would call territorial, but in a tank, there's not a lot of territory," Beasley explains. Fights and biting can occur. A bigger tank out back can hold about five small turtles for "playtime" during good weather. If a turtle begins biting, though, it is immediately removed and taken to "time-out."

The Turtle Hospital on Topsail is virtually unique. There are few other turtles-only facilities in the United States, though a number of facilities include turtles among the marine life they treat. "This *is* a hospital," Beasley explains. So visiting hours are limited to two or maybe two and a half hours a day five days a week for three months during the summer, plus the Autumn With Topsail festival weekend in October. Even the short hours can be difficult on the turtles. "You look at these turtles after people have been gawking. They're exhausted. They go to the far side of their tanks."

The turtles are here to be nursed back to health, after all, in hopes they can be returned to the sea. In time, most will. They have been rushed here with everything from concussions to infections to severed flippers, serious conditions requiring treatment here or surgery elsewhere or often both. Some do

Families line up during the Autumn With Topsail festival to see giant sea turtles. Here at the Turtle Hospital, loggerheads and other injured or sick sea turtles are treated until they can be released back to the ocean. Visiting hours are necessarily limited, and long lines are common. But so are the oohs and aahs of anyone who sees the turtles.

not survive. Most heal sufficiently to be released within perhaps a year or so. "It is very fulfilling to get a turtle that's almost died and be able to return it," Beasley says with feeling. She has no doubt spoken the same words on hundreds, perhaps thousands, of occasions—and meant them every time.

Most of the residents are loggerheads, along with green and Kemp's ridley sea turtles. All are federally protected because of dwindling numbers. All are huge, or can be. Loggerheads, which can live 100 years, sometimes weigh 400 or 500 pounds in adulthood.

The hospital has 20 or more turtles at a time, crowding it to capacity and beyond. Back in the mid-1990s, authorities said not to worry, the small hospital would never have more than three to five turtles. What happened? "People never reported sick turtles or injured turtles before," Beasley explains. "They just died." Once the hospital opened, the real numbers became known. Since 1998, the hospital has averaged 19 admissions a year, hitting a peak of 27 in 2004.

On a typical day, when the hospital is caring for 17 turtles, Beasley introduces a few being nursed back to health.

- Wendy, a loggerhead, was brought in by Wendy Cluse, a 2001 summer intern who is now the assistant sea-turtle coordinator for the state of North Carolina. The turtle, spotted swimming in circles in the ocean, was only the size of a 50-cent piece yet had an infection the size of a marble over the left eye. To make matters worse, her right eye was sealed.

- Brunswick III, found in Brunswick County, had her left rear flipper nearly severed, most likely by a boat propeller. She had lost considerable blood. Through cutting-edge surgery at North Carolina State University, ligaments and tendons were manufactured from catgut for her. Brunswick III, about 10 or 12 years old, now weighs about 150 pounds.

- Briggy, a Kemp's ridley, was found entangled in fishing wire and missing a flipper. Briggy was found at Brigantine Island, near Atlantic City, New Jersey, and flown down to Topsail.

- Splash, a loggerhead found by a Wilmington schoolboy, was a "floater," a turtle with serious breathing problems. The hospital doesn't know why; it may have come from being caught in a fishing net. The grade-school boy has remained as interested as the staff, begging his mother to bring him in every few weeks.

The hospital, which operates year-round, is named for Jean's daughter, Karen, who died in 1991 while still in her 20s. Karen's insurance paid for the hospital. Donations from corporations and the 20,000 to 25,000 visitors who see the turtles each year help pay for food, medical supplies, operating costs, and $25,000 in outside veterinary costs. Fund-raising is a constant. T-shirts and other souvenirs are sold in a tent in front of the building.

The hospital is a fitting legacy. Karen Beasley organized the island's turtle-watch program to protect nesting turtles and their hatchlings. The Topsail Turtle Project continues the work through volunteers who collectively walk every mile of the island's 26-mile beach every morning from May through August. They look for the bulldozer-like tracks of sea turtles—and the nests they portend.

Loggerhead turtles come ashore three to five times during a nesting year, leaving an average of 120 eggs each time. Volunteers cordon off the nests to keep tourists at a distance and even move the nests if necessary. Sixty days later, the baby turtles should be ready for their walk to the sea. Volunteers line their path in encouragement.

Natural predators abound, however. If the tiny two-ounce baby turtles hatch and make it out of the nests, they must escape ghost crabs on their race to the sea. In the sea, they must hide from both birds and fish. Man is a killing force as well. Oceanfront lighting can disorient nesting mothers at the very beginning or lead hatchlings on a fatal trip away from the sea—one reason for the Topsail Turtle Project's "Dig the Dark" education program.

All seven species of sea turtles are declining worldwide, Beasley emphasizes. "We have to stand up for the turtles," she says. "They have no voice. We are their voice." Nature kills many, but so does man. The causes range from toxins to debris to boats to fishing hooks to fishing nets to dwindling food sources. "We are consumers of the planet," Beasley says. "We live on this planet as if we have another."

So the baby-turtle project is not as critical as the hospital work, Beasley says. "Hatchlings are wonderful, but this is what's really important." Her words at first seem harsh. It's simply a numbers game. Adult turtles are more important than hatchlings. Only one baby in 5,000 or even 10,000 reaches adulthood, which takes 20 or 30 years for a loggerhead. The odds seem astronomical. Keeping alive an injured sea turtle—any sea turtle, but especially an adult—becomes paramount.

Topsail's first turtle in need of care came in with a head injury in the fall of 1995, two years before the hospital was built. Fittingly, the turtle was named Lucky. Beasley and Sandy Sly, a volunteer with the turtle-nesting program, took Lucky to the North Carolina State University veterinary school for treatment. They found they weren't finished, Sly says; the hospital informed them they were taking the turtle back afterward. They ended up taking her to St. Augustine, Florida, for the winter. SeaWorld returned Lucky when Topsail's weather got warm again.

Meanwhile, a board member of the sea-turtle project volunteered his property. The first Topsail turtles were treated there in a child's swimming pool. "When the weather got cold, we had to put a tent over it and run a heater out to it," Beasley says, showing a picture. When winter came, they continued taking turtles down to Florida facilities.

Jean Beasley started and watches over the Karen Beasley Sea Turtle Rescue and Rehabilitation Center. Her late daughter organized the island's turtle-watch program to protect nesting turtles and their hatchlings. That work continues under the auspices of the hospital. Every morning from May through August, volunteers walk Topsail's 26 miles of beaches looking for turtle nests.

The next summer, Sly says, they got Huffy, a loggerhead with deep wounds from being hit by a boat propeller. Huffy was taken to Florida, flown in a Coast Guard C-130 plane to Orlando. "It got lots of media coverage," she says. "She was a celebrity." Brought back when Topsail's weather was warm, Huffy was ultimately released in the summer of 1997.

Beasley and her fellow turtle crusaders, it was clear, needed a facility.

Topsail Beach offered a piece of property fronting on Carolina Boulevard and backing up to Topsail Sound, next to a marina. The town legally couldn't give it away but leased it for one dollar a year. The Turtle Hospital was to be built in 1996, but Hurricanes Bertha and Fran hit the island that year.

"There was no way we could even talk about building a turtle hospital when people lost their homes," Beasley says.

The 900-square-foot hospital finally opened on November 7, 1997. Inside are tanks, medical equipment, supplies, an examining table, and a water-exchange system that continually pumps water from the sound into the tanks and then back. During the winter, the water first is pumped into outdoor reservoir tanks and heated to 75 degrees.

The hospital and the Topsail Turtle Project get help from volunteers and student interns. There are perhaps 650 volunteers, their commitments ranging from the occasional to the complete. Seven hospital interns work each summer, plus four each fall and four each spring. Theirs is a learning experience—some students gain college credit—and a bonding experience they never forget. It also is undeniably hard work. The hospital's Web site (www.seaturtlehospital.org) gives an idea.

A DAY IN THE LIFE: TWENTY OR SO SEA TURTLES. That's a lot to care for. Different diets, and personalities. Different medicines, vitamins and wound care regimes. Continuous monitoring of intake and output, water quality and temperature; flushing and cleaning and redirecting of water pipes. Laundry, laundry, laundry.

Our volunteers handle these duties and many more every day, changing hats from feeders and cleaners and medical care givers to ambassadors and educators, administrators and fund raisers.

The first volunteers arrive each morning around 7 A.M. to begin food and medication preparation, followed soon after by a highly dedicated team of folks who will proceed to:

Feed each turtle according to needs and yes, wants. (They can be choosy eaters, too.)

Drain and clean each tank.

Administer to the special needs of each turtle.

Refill each tank.

Wash, dry, fold and stack towels, repeat, repeat, repeat.

Physically prepare the building for visitors in the afternoon.

Open to the public.

Introduce the public to the patients and the facility.

Close to the public.

Clean up, scoop tank. . . .

It's often difficult and hot work, not to mention dirty and smelly. The rewards are plentiful and where you find them: the look in the turtles' eyes, their eager and able return to the sea.

It takes between six months and four years of treatment before a turtle can be released to the sea. Each is checked thoroughly and marked before release.

Releases usually come in the spring and fall. The hospital no longer publicizes the dates. Crowds simply became too large. Beasley shows a picture: a throng of people is lined up the width of the beach behind a rope, as if being held back from celebrities at the Academy Awards. Another throng similarly was being held on the other side of the release area, outside the camera's range. There were 1,200 spectators that day. For another release, 2,500 people showed up, a few of whom wrestled with the large but vulnerable turtles once they reached the water. Beasley and the police agreed the event had gotten too large.

School classes are still invited to watch releases, however. Beasley, a former teacher and school administrator, believes education is one of the hospital's principal missions. That's one reason a larger hospital is needed: the original is too dangerous for school groups. More space is needed for turtles and workers alike—for a classroom, an eating area, showers, larger bathrooms. There is little room to build on the Topsail Beach property.

The hospital has been given land on the mainland portion of Surf City, a location that might also require fewer turtle evacuations for approaching storms. Access issues remain with that property, though. If Beasley cannot move the hospital, she will try to expand it as much as possible. "We love it here," she says. "Topsail Beach has been wonderful for us." She would not be thinking of moving were it not for the space.

Beasley tells a story from the early days, before the hospital was built. Hurricane Fran was approaching. Beasley and volunteers evacuated the turtles from the island. She was still finishing up duties before leaving when a parent called. The family's children were worried sick over the turtles. "Tell them," Beasley assured the parent, "the turtles are all off the island. They're all safe. But start worrying about me."

She was kidding, of course. But the island does need Beasley and the many volunteers of the Turtle Hospital and project.

So do the tourists.

So do the turtles.

CHAPTER EIGHTEEN

Songwriters

Chris Pappalardo no longer tells time the way he did on the mainland.

He uses a Topsail Island watch.

The watch was made by a friend, and Chris uses it especially when he's writing. It has no hands, which would seem to hinder the traditional time-telling function. Instead, grains of sand, a few small beach rocks, and even tiny black shark teeth all float free inside the watch crystal. It is a reminder of the pace of the island.

If there is a symbol of the island, it may well be the Topsail Island watch.

But if there is an advertisement for the island, it may well be the traveling troubadours known as Waterline. Pappalardo, a guitarist-singer-songwriter, and his buddy Jim Ellis, a

Calling all weekend warriors, summer
  Tom Sawyers
Adventuring down to the sea
This here's a special place, I'll give you a taste
But take this advice from me
Forget your rooftop rack, with all the bags you
  packed
You've got to simplify your act
You need a lesson in a state of mind

Here on an island you can't help smilin'
It's a feeling you get when you cross that bridge
And leave the world behind
Here on an island you lose track of time
It's therapy for your mind
On an island

From "Here on an Island," written by Jim Ellis
about Topsail Island, performed by Waterline

keyboardist-singer-songwriter, not only chose the island as a home but as material as well.

Now, they sing the magic of Topsail.

The story of the North Topsail Beach duo goes back to the early 1990s, when they met in Chris's hometown of Richmond, Virginia. He was a music student at Virginia Commonwealth University and Jim a business student at the University of Richmond. The two soon were playing in a three-person band. They knew it didn't have "the X-factor," as the two call it. "We played a gig at the Flood Zone in 1992, and Dave Matthews opened up for *us*," Chris says, smiling at the notion of one of rock's biggest names-in-the-making playing second fiddle. "I said, 'They have it.' We didn't."

Chris headed to Nashville, taking college classes in the music industry and touring with guitarist Sonny Landreth. Jim stayed in Richmond as a banker, "doing the regular day job," he says. "And one day I called up Chris and said, 'Let's play music.' He was at that point, too."

They gave it another try, moving to Wilmington. It was on their way there in December 1995, driving down Interstate 40, that their band name came to them. The Dire Straits tune "Down to the Waterline" came on the radio just as they were driving to the sea. They knew.

What they didn't know was that Waterline's very first performance would have meaning, too. The first gig they ever played was in Topsail, Jim says. A musician called up and asked if they could fill in for him. They could, they did, and in March 1996, Waterline debuted at The Offshore Grill, a small restaurant in Topsail Beach that has since closed. It was a good opening before the locals, though the big summer crowds had not arrived yet.

From 1996 until 1999, Waterline played small clubs on

the Carolina coast from Beaufort down to Myrtle Beach, doing James Taylor songs, Jimmy Buffett songs, and a few of their own. Topsail was a frequent stop, usually at Surf City's One-Eyed Parrot, which since has become Buddy's Crab House and Oyster Bar. Topsail's laid-back atmosphere was a good fit for the two musicians, who never came to a performance with a set list, preferring to play the songs that seemed right at the moment. "That lends itself to this area. . . . The gig was eight to midnight. We played till one, we'd play till two," Chris says. "How late didn't matter. That's really true of this place."

Waterline put out its first compact disk, *Stranded*, in 1999. Jim wrote two Topsail-inspired songs. One, the title track, conveys being happily trapped in an inlet near the island:

> *Stuck on a sandbar*
> *Tide's rollin' in*
> *Been here for hours*
> *Feels like I just put in*
>
> *Waterline risin'*
> *I'll float before long*
> *Think I'll drop my anchor*
> *And stay gone*
>
> *I'm stranded where I want to be*
> *I'm grounded in the middle of the sea*
> *Where the water is warm and I can be alone*
> *Stranded*
> *May never go home*
>
> *Rather grow old here*
> *Watchin' the waves*

Than on dry land
The rest of my days

Some call me crazy
But I know I'm right
Tradin' creature comforts
For simple pleasures of life

I'm stranded where I want to be
I'm grounded in the middle of the sea
Where the water is warm and I can be alone
Stranded
May never go home

If "Stranded" is the yin of Topsail, "Vacation Wasteland" is the yang. The song describes the devastation visited upon the island, especially North Topsail Beach, by Hurricanes Bertha and Fran in 1996:

There's a steady beat made by tires on the
    causeway
The summer heat is risin' up from the road
Roll down the windows
Smell the salt air
And look out at the blue water below

Yes, I remember those holiday vacations
Here with the seagulls and castles of sand
They've blown away by storms of the season
Leaving only
A vacation wasteland

They've got shrimp boats backed up on the highway

People walkin' the streets tryin' to find what they
      own
Stairways steppin' up to nowhere
They can't go home

'Cause a wall of water came barrelin' through this
      beach town
Homes on the frontline were too weak to stand
Windows boarded up
Shops closed down
All that remains
Is vacation wasteland

At the end of the land
And the edge of the sea
In the wind and waves
Is where we all want to be
Till the hurricanes level
Dreams in the sand
And all that remains
Is vacation wasteland

Shortly after their CD came out, the two put Waterline in mothballs. They were doing okay, Jim says, but they were far from a big hit.

Chris and his wife, Shannon, moved back to Nashville, then to Asheville, North Carolina, where he managed a music store for three years. In 2002, they moved to Virginia Beach, and he managed a piano store for three more years. He was financially successful, but it wasn't right. "We never went to the beach," he says. "We didn't like the people, the energy. We couldn't find a church." Meanwhile, Chris had gone back on the road with guitarist Lee Roy Parnell, who sometimes played before huge crowds. It still didn't feel quite right.

For those six years, Waterline performed only one weekend a month, maybe two. "I'd made two businesses very success-ful, but I never made Waterline successful," Chris says. That was what he cared about. Jim felt the same way. By day, he was a salesman for a Wilmington graphic-design firm, and he was playing and even recording with a number of musicians. "Nothing had the X-factor like we had," he says.

Chris remembers a moment when the two were playing on Topsail. "In July '04, we played the Beach House Marina. We looked at each other like, 'What are we doing? This is what we want.'"

Jim already knew he wanted Topsail Island. He and his wife, Dawn, had started spending weekends in North Topsail Beach in 2003. They liked it so much—"I'd get here on the weekend," Jim says, "and I didn't want to leave the island at all"—they bought a bigger house and moved there in 2004. Living on Topsail was worth the commute to Wilmington.

When Jim called Chris later in 2004 with a line on a house near his own in North Topsail Beach, the Pappalardos jumped on it. "It's like coming home," Chris says of Topsail. "It's the anti-Wrightsville Beach. It's much more laid-back."

Even before the move, Waterline had reunited. Using Chris and Shannon's contacts, they got top-notch backing and producing for their second CD, recording in Virginia Beach, Asheville, and Lafayette, Louisiana. *Long Goners* was released in 2005, a month before the Pappalardos moved to Topsail. The title refers to Waterline's six years away from their music and from their hearts. The symbolic cover art shows the two musicians on the beach—walking away and then, on the re-verse side, coming back. They were indeed back.

The group is still not big-time. But die-hard fans—the

Jim Ellis and Chris Pappalardo, guitar in case, walk their home beach. The North Topsail Beach duo performs as Waterline. More than a little of Topsail Island washes over their music. Jim explains the island's allure: "You notice things more. I notice where the sun rises and sets. Nowhere else I've lived have I ever thought of noticing where the sun sets." Chris adds, "The minute I cross that bridge, I don't care what I've been doing. It slaps you in the face, and you can't ignore that." (Shannon Pappalardo)

self-named "Waterheads"—now number more than 600. Thanks to the Internet, CD sales come from as far away as Japan and the Netherlands. The two play 90 to 120 times a year, including as many Topsail dates as reasonable. During the summers, they have played once a week at The Mainsail's Commodore Room in Surf City and once or twice a month at Skully's Pub and Grub in Topsail Beach.

Their music is tough to pigeonhole. Call it country rock with a Buffett accent or maybe a Bruce Hornsby tilt. Their Web site (www.waterlinemusic.com) likens their sound to

Jackson Browne and the Eagles and their first album to James Taylor and Buffett. Chris says, "It's not beach music—you can't shag to it. And we're not Jimmy Buffett." For the time being, the band is considering calling its music "coastal rock."

Even better might be "Topsail rock."

Their identity as a Topsail band is growing. Daily newspapers in Wilmington and Jacksonville have featured Waterline, as has *Topsail Magazine*. In 2006, Waterline began adding large festivals to its tours of small clubs. "Now our goal is to go out to these festivals and express this place," Chris says. Trouble is, he adds, they hate leaving the island. But that makes the return home sweeter. "The minute I cross that bridge, I don't care what I've been doing," Chris says. "It slaps you in the face, and you can't ignore that."

Their third CD will be the first to be substantially Topsail-inspired. The two write on their front porches and at the beach and even talk into recorders driving down the roads of Topsail. Songs in hand, they meet to work out the performances. They don't lack for inspiration. Topsail has The Magic—or, as the two might call it, the X-factor. "I can look at the sun going down every day. Out the other window, I can look at the ocean," Chris says. Up and down the East Coast, he has never found a better spot. He describes how, on July 4, 2005, "the busiest beach day of the year, I'm throwing a ball with my Lab on the beach. Where else can you do that? I'm flying a kite."

Chris thinks the small island will stay small. The mainland will boom, but "this island, it can't grow so much. I'm not going to have a BrewThru up the block. It's not going to become Nags Head. It can't." He knows the Outer Banks. His father lived in Nags Head until he visited his son. Then he moved to Topsail, too.

Jim, who has written most of the band's songs so far,

agrees. "Topsail, I think, far exceeds any of the other islands. I've written songs about it. You cross the bridge and get a feeling of relaxation. You leave the world behind. You cross the swing bridge and your blood pressure drops. I haven't lost that feeling in the years living up here either." Jim pauses. "It's everything about the island. You notice things more. I notice where the sun rises and sets. Nowhere else I've lived have I ever thought of noticing where the sun sets."

He tried to convey that in "Here on an Island," the first song he wrote after moving to Topsail. Waterline recorded a demo of the tune and made it available to fans as a New Year's 2006 present.

> *I'm counting my blessings daily, I was slowly*
> *fading*
> *When I saw it all so clear*
> *I clocked my 9-to-5, fought rush-hour drives*
> *For a two-week vacation each year*
> *But it took that salt in my skin and that ocean*
> *wind*
> *To breathe some life into me again*
> *Now it's holiday all of the time*
>
> *Here on an island you can't help smilin'*
> *It's a feeling you get when you cross that bridge*
> *And leave the world behind*
> *Here on an island you lose track of time*
> *It's therapy for your mind*
> *On an island*
>
> *You can shake your head and make your bed on*
> *the mainland*

Yeah that's a perfectly civilized game plan
But what a shame man

Here on an island you can't help smilin'
It's a feeling you get when you cross that bridge
And leave the world behind
Here on an island you lose track of time
It's therapy for your mind
On an island

"That's a very autobiographical sort of song," Jim says. "Coming across the bridge, that was one of the first lines that came to me: 'When you cross that bridge and leave the world behind.' " He put as much of the Topsail experience as he could into it. "There's nothing better than being able to look out the back deck and see the sound and then walking two blocks to the beach." He pauses. "Most people get two weeks of this. I'm so lucky to be living it."

Yes, the two weeks made it into the song as well.

Topsail is not for everyone, Chris says. The island's laid-back attitude and less-than-strict adherence to the clock can be maddening to employers. "Employees may show up late one day or not show up at all. And they don't apologize either. 'The waves are good,' " Chris says. That means it is time to surf instead of time to work. " 'The waves are good.' And they look at you like you should understand. Of course they wouldn't work: The waves are good." That goes for visitors, too. "You're either going to fall in love or you're never coming back," Chris says. Try going to a restaurant. "You want your food in 10 minutes? Maybe. *Maybe*. Are the waves good?"

That's fine for Waterline. Jim and Chris have reevaluated what's important to them. Their music. The island. The slower pace.

"When you cross that bridge, don't honk at me," Chris says, smiling. "You're on our time now."

Call it Topsail Island time.

And only one type of watch will do.

CHAPTER NINETEEN

The Point

O$_n$ *a warm September evening in 2005, the Topsail Beach Town Commission met before a full house.* Shorts-wearing residents filled row upon row of chairs. Two or three went out to smoke cigarettes and came back in, but most sat patiently through the administrative matters. Several rose to congratulate the board for how it had handled Hurricane Ophelia the previous week—evacuating endangered areas before the storm, getting cleanup under way quickly afterward, and applying for federal money for beach restoration.

But most were waiting to see what the elected leaders could do, and would do, to maintain the island as they had come to know it.

The issues involved growth, as they always do on Topsail, and the board quickly disposed of one, agreeing to buy a boat ramp if a deal could be made. Private boat ramps open to the public have been swallowed up by developers. This was an opportunity—probably the last opportunity—to keep a public ramp. The board hoped grant money would cover the cost. If not, taxes would have to.

The thornier issue, though, was The Point and what it stands for.

The Point is as beautiful a piece of land as any on Topsail and more important than most. Lying southernmost on the island, the unspoiled land wraps around from the sound to the ocean. Technically, The Point lies beyond Serenity Point, the southernmost development, but often the two names are used interchangeably. At The Point, nature shows its artistry: water, birds, fish, sand, sun, breezes. Beachgoers explore The Point, sometimes stopping to set up a fishing pole or two, sometimes helping their children or grandchildren find shells, sometimes walking out into the clear water of the sound to a sand bar. And then just sitting.

The Point has been growing. Call it nature's land swap. Since New Topsail Inlet opened in 1738, the island has migrated more than six miles to the south, according to the Coastal Hazards Information Clearinghouse at Western Carolina University. The northern end of the island is slowly being taken back by the sea, but the southern end benefits with growing acreage. Developers want those acres. They have approached the several owners with increasingly attractive offers. The owners—in some cases island families going back generations—have resisted. But millions of dollars await them when they change their minds.

The town of 500 residents has an annual budget of only $1.7 million and cannot afford the 125 to 135 acres of prime land. The Topsail Beach board tried designating the land as a conservation preserve but backed down when confronted by

The Point

The unspoiled acreage of The Point wraps around Topsail's southern end from the ocean to Topsail Sound. Inland, birds and small animals claim a home in the marshy forest. At water's edge, beachgoers walk the sandy expanse of The Point, sometimes setting up a fishing pole, sometimes stooping to find shells, sometimes walking out into the clear water of the sound and sitting on a sand bar.

the owners' lawyer. So, on the warm evening in September 2005, the board contracted with the North Carolina Coastal Land Trust, which had a good track record of finding grants for land like this. It would survey and appraise The Point, then, if feasible, find money to buy it for the town. If it could accomplish that, nearly everyone would be happy.

If not, Topsail might lose a symbolic battle for its soul.

The Point has been national news, a lengthy article landing on the front page of the *Wall Street Journal* in December 2005. The four decks of headline told the story: "Hurricane Warning," read the first headline. "On Topsail Island, Storms

Each year, the magnificent beach at The Point grows. Ocean and inlet currents deposit acres upon acres of sand on the island's southern end. Indeed, since New Topsail Inlet opened in 1738, the island has migrated more than six miles to the south.

Fuel Battle Over Right to Build," was next, followed by "Foes Cite Endless Repair Bills and Fears of Weakening Mainland Flood Defenses," and finally, "Beach Neighbors Turn Frosty."

The article detailed a story well known to islanders. M. A. Boryk and partners bought two dozen acres at the southern end of Topsail Island at auction in the early 1960s. They and their families became wealthy by building and selling homes. Over the years, Mother Nature has given them an additional 125 acres—assessed at $30 million—in the form of property-extending sand brought by storms, currents, and winds. Boryk's heirs believe it is theirs to sell as they please, though a "Save The Point" group of neighbors sprouted up in opposition. Boryk's daughter, Annette Oppegaard, wife of former mayor Kip Oppegaard, told the *Journal*, "We know that it's a fragile area, and the Lord gives and the Lord takes away. But if someone gave you something, you would probably want to use it to do what's best for your children and grandchildren." The heirs say they are willing to sell the land for conservation—for a while.

Garth Boyd, one of the town commissioners for Topsail Beach, says The Point is merely the best example of a town problem. "All of our land is becoming extraordinarily valuable. It's a nice dilemma to have. To people on the south end, . . . they deserve to cash in. However, we have something at the south end that is extraordinary on the East Coast."

The Point at sunset is a sight for the ages.

It is no wonder developers are smitten. Everyone is. There is a feeling of almost complete isolation, yet a sense one is at home. The day draws to a close. Sitting on the rear deck of one of the southernmost Serenity Point homes, a visitor instantly gets it. The home belongs to Woody and Susan Tucker, who instinctively save outward-facing seats for guests.

The view is of a verdant expanse natural and unspoiled, the likes of which one rarely sees. Comparisons are difficult. The land is part marsh, part maritime forest, part buffer from storms. Susan Tucker says it is marshy, overgrown, not land to be walked upon. Wax myrtle (or bayberry) trees thrive here, along with live oaks and natural grasses. So do cedars most certainly born from bird droppings that contained the seeds.

It is a solid, rough-looking expanse from up here on the deck, a natural habitat for birds that can be seen and animals that cannot. The Tuckers hear cardinals, doves, purple finches, blue jays, and mockingbirds, all drawn by the freshwater lagoon at The Point. There are red-winged blackbirds, gulls, plovers, and even pelicans, known locally as "the Topsail

Air Force." The Tuckers are almost convinced The Point is a turning basin for pelicans, so often do they see them soar south along the community road, reach The Point, then turn around and head back north. A hawk sometimes hunts the area, too. There are feral cats, raccoons, and opossums.

To the right, the sun is about to go down over Topsail Sound. From the left, a warm, melodious sound comes from over the Atlantic Ocean. A ship at sea? A foghorn? The howl of the northeast wind? Any would seem possible, but ocean charts show a device called a sound buoy. It is part of the Serenity Point symphony.

Off in the dark green expanse toward the ocean, someone has mounted a birdhouse on a very tall pole. It stands alone in the dusk. Purple martins are supposed to be lured there to eat mosquitoes. But with decks built off the backs of so many homes, the birdhouse now may be too close for the martins. Instead, a hummingbird uses it as a base for occasional flights to visit the homeowners.

Nothing else interferes with the view. There is no other sign that a soul has ever been here before.

Straight ahead, on the far side of the green expanse, is the huge new beach deposited by Mother Nature and fought over by man. For the time being, Mother Nature and the island's inhabitants are in a truce, however uneasy. It seemingly could fall apart at any time.

But sitting here as the sun slowly drops, one hopes serenity continues at The Point.

CHAPTER TWENTY

Mayberry Tomorrow

The owner of the Beach Shop and Grill saw it almost as soon as he took over the restaurant for the summer season of 2002. "Not long after I bought, real estate went up 25 percent a year," Jeffrey Stewart Price says. "The secret got out. The cat got out of the bag."

Price means the allure of Topsail, "The Magic," the Mayberry. At Topsail, vacationers and an ever-increasing number of baby-boomer retirees can still find the family beach they remember. Real-estate offices have been flooded for years. Construction companies work overtime. The 21st-century growth in visitors and the demand for property have been staggering.

In recent years, the Hedgecock Lumber

Sea gulls and beach graders are two constants on Topsail Island. The small barrier island is battered and reshaped by storms and ocean currents. Maintaining the allure of Topsail requires periodic beach rebuilding. "That God-given resource out there," one official says, "is why people are coming—and we've got to protect it."

Company and the Florida Apartments near Price's restaurant were both sold, to be replaced by high-priced homes. Price says the town government has things under control with building codes and height restrictions. He believes Topsail Beach made a mistake by not having a sewer system but agrees septic tanks have limited growth. Still, he says, the growth has been obvious. As a restaurant and gift-shop owner, Price is fine with it, as long as the atmosphere of the island remains. "I'd just as soon build a high-rise down here," he says, laughing at the impossibility. "But people would kill me."

The specter of growth is always the issue on Topsail. A few blocks away, Robin Orr is part-owner and manager of the Jolly Roger Pier and the adjacent motel once owned by his

206

father, Lewis. "Everybody wants to stop development—the blow-up-the-bridge mentality," he says. Don't let anyone else on the island, in other words. "Some of it's well intended. They don't want to change the climate." He grins. "But they didn't feel that way initially."

Call it the island irony: the flood of visitors and new residents threatens the very way of life that brought them to this quiet little spot in the first place.

"We've become the 'got-miners,'" says Topsail Beach mayor Butch Parrish with a knowing laugh. "I've got mine, now you stay out." As real-estate values have skyrocketed, the quaintness of Topsail has come under attack. Small cottages are sold, razed, and replaced by the largest duplexes allowable under building codes. Owners of small businesses and shops in Topsail Beach and Surf City can make more money by selling than by staying and offering their services summer after summer. "That's one of the troubles," Parrish says. "I don't know what to do about it."

Parrish is sitting in the Beach Shop and Grill, talking while eating breakfast. "Nobody could afford to build this building today—buy the land, build the building," he says. "You can't afford to do it unless you have Wrightsville Beach volume." And nobody, Parrish says as if the point is not clear, wants that.

Barry Newsome, who has been part of the island for more than half a century, is confident that Topsail Beach will always maintain its small-town atmosphere. But he worries a little that "some of the enchantment will be gone, which happens anywhere. People find a good thing and love it to death." Newsome remembers the first party, an oyster roast, that he and his wife attended upon moving to the island full-time. "One of the old-timers said, 'If I had my way, at the IGA we'd just put up a sign that says, No Right Turn.'" If crowds must come to the island, in other words, keep them up in Surf City, not down here in Topsail Beach.

Garth Boyd sympathizes. "We're loving it to death. Human nature is, 'As soon as I have my place, let's put up a tall gate.'" But the Topsail Beach commission member says he and his fellow officials don't have the right to quash private-property rights.

Boyd wrote a newsletter article in 2005 in which he cited seven signs of growth, including the closing of two boat ramps and "the slow but steady stream of older homes lumbering down the road and off the island to less expensive lots; the empty lots left behind soon to be replaced by much larger, modern homes." The town's total property value had leapt from $213 million in 2003 to $396 million the next year. More staggering growth was in store, and for just one reason: the law of supply and demand. Money from around the country was funneling onto the tiny island, Boyd wrote. "This disturbing trend points out the dire need for us to patronize and support our existing businesses if we are to preserve the charm and convenience" of the town.

Up the road, Surf City faces similar challenges. Mom-and-pop shop owners can make more by selling their properties than by running their businesses.

After the turn of the 21st century, the town saw a 30 to 40 percent increase in real-estate investment, the growth fueled by the decline of the stock market and by low home-building interest rates, Doug Medlin says. Medlin has served more than two decades on the Surf City council and has also served a term as mayor. In 2005, Medlin explains, the council came up with a partial solution to keep small businesses on the island: the concept of an "urban waterfront." While most of Surf City has a height restriction of 48 feet—or four stories—developers can apply for what amounts to another level in the area near the marina by putting in retail space on the lowest floor.

The compromise brought attacks from both sides. The first to take advantage of the new regulations, the Grande Meridian Resort, complained in early 2006 that it needed three feet more than the new 60-foot maximum. The council denied the request. But that hardly quieted residents who complained at a meeting that even a 60-foot resort would destroy the town's character. Inez Bradt, whose weekly "Pender Pride" column is published in local newspapers, was emphatic, according to the *Topsail Voice*. "I've been here 41 years and enough is enough. We need to put a limit." The resort's representative, Mark Yow, descended from Surf City founder Edgar Yow, said that while residents are entitled to their opinions, "I think we've been a leader in the community since day one. The project meets every ecological requirement you can imagine. We've built a lush little oasis here. There are things the town needs and tax base is one of them."

The battle over the future of the lush little island oasis continues.

Zander Guy, Surf City's mayor, sits in his real-estate office and sees inevitable growth. Look up and down the East Coast, Guy says. Moreover, growth is necessary for the area's young people, who go away to school, then want to return—only to find there are few jobs. Increasingly, people are settling as year-round residents. "If you can visualize Surf City [in 2000] in winter, you had to hold a flashlight to see your way around." Since then, the influx of new residents has led to the hiring of a town recreational director and the opening in 2006 of a 17,000-square-foot community center off the island.

Guy sees a need to meld the two forces that always seem to be at odds: growth and the character of Topsail Island. "That God-given resource out there," he says, gesturing toward the ocean and the beach, "is why people are coming—and we've got to protect it."

That means everything from expensive beach renourishment programs to limiting character-changing development. For Guy, one of the major players in the island's real-estate market, the latter in particular seems ironic. "As you get older," he says, "sometimes you see things through different eyes." It's up to community leaders to protect the island for future generations. He says the current Surf City council is one of the most visionary boards he's seen.

Surf City is in the enviable position of having a growing tax base, at least part of which will not directly affect the island's character. Over the years, the town has slowly expanded across the Intracoastal Waterway onto the mainland and down S.R. 210 to U.S. 17, which is becoming prime commercial property.

At North Topsail Beach, which has come late to the development game, some issues are different. Builders are not knocking down quaint old cottages before putting up duplexes and large homes. There are no quaint old cottages, or at least not many. Hurricanes took care of most that were here. Even more than the other two towns, low-lying North Topsail seems to be at the mercy of the elements. Every so often, the sea decides to reclaim what belongs to it.

Other issues are similar. The maximum allowable building height is fought over here as well. As elected officials replace one another, the question of whether the town should have a 45- or 50-foot maximum is revisited periodically.

Meanwhile, large new homes keep appearing in North Topsail. The value of the land goes higher and higher. "Twelve years ago, it was the best-kept secret in North Carolina. Now, it's not a secret anymore," says Loraine Carbone, town clerk and, on three separate occasions, acting town manager. She

The future of Topsail Island is both promising and uncertain.
Keeping the unique small-town charm while providing a welcome to
ever-increasing numbers will test the island's leaders.

picks up a copy of the *Topsail Voice* newspaper and flips to the
real-estate ads. A five-bedroom oceanfront home in North
Topsail is listed for $2 million. An oceanfront lot—just the
lot—is listed for $1 million.

Carbone knew the 2006 real-estate reassessments and increasing tax bills would hit both the elderly and the young
hard. When Onslow County released its 2006 assessments,
residents who thought they had braced for the worst found
they had not. Property values, on average, had increased 377
percent in just six years. One parcel on New River Inlet Road
had been assessed at $150,000 in 2000; by 2006, the assess-
ment was $1.245 million. Even North Topsail alderman Dan
Tuman told the *Jacksonville Daily News* he underestimated
the impact on his own home. "I was anticipating that the

revaluation was going to double. But I was shocked to see it had quadrupled. I suspect a lot of people will be stunned with their new revaluation. It will take them awhile to come down off the ceiling." Even lowered tax rates did not fully compensate. The island has become a more expensive place to live.

Newsome, one of the civic leaders down the island in Topsail Beach, knows that. He was born in 1932 and began visiting the island in 1952. Now retired, he lives year-round here. "People my age, 90 percent of us, if we were not here already, we couldn't afford to come here. We laugh: If we died tomorrow and they see what it's worth, it will be sold tomorrow."

Despite the problems on Topsail, optimism runs high. After all, many of the problems come because the island is, in essence, too desirable.

Surf City mayor Guy keeps returning to a few themes in his vision of the island. First, protect the ocean, the beach, and the town's character; that's what everything else is based on. Second, encourage small businesses in the island portion of his town while attracting bigger commercial enterprises to the mainland. And third, "the ideal thing to happen, and it won't happen in my lifetime, is one municipality," Guy says. Instead of three towns, the island should be one. Consolidating the governments would avoid duplication of services and save money on water, police and fire services, and dozens of smaller items. Moreover, it would give Topsail greater clout in dealing with the federal government and seeking funds to keep the fragile island safe.

Topsail Beach mayor Butch Parrish—not aware of Guy's comments—says the consolidation proposal often is made by outsiders but that locals, knowing the differences among the towns, simply roll their eyes. Guy is no outsider, however, and at least limited cooperation may be on its way. Topsail Beach, facing water shortages, asked Surf City for help, and the two towns worked for an agreement. Moreover, many of the island's current politicians, including the affable Parrish, have been more conciliatory than some predecessors.

Besides, there is a commonality of large interests, if not small ones. The entire island is minuscule—just 15 square miles—and there can't be much sense in competing against itself. A new consolidated town of Topsail Island—or whatever it might be named—would have an advantage in dealing with increased growth pressures in the 21st century, in everything from zoning restrictions to marketing to hitting up the feds for beach money.

Preserving Topsail's atmosphere will take creative thinking. However the island is structured, Topsail Beach's new 20-year land-use plan may offer a mission statement for the entire island. It is a vision of the island today and tomorrow: "Topsail Beach is a beautiful, family beach that will be relatively crime free, economically sound and a leader of coastal communities in environmental protection and beach preservation. We will maintain a high quality of life and relaxed atmosphere that other towns will try to duplicate. We know that the reason for our success is simple: It is our people, our community, who share the vision of the Town's bright future."

Ultimately, that vision and the work it takes to uphold it are what will have to protect the island in the face of threats from nature and man.

The islanders and most of Topsail's guests share the vision, as they have since they arrived and began to build well over a half-century ago. It is a vision of pristine beaches and clean waters, of small cottages and scattered shops, of friendly neighbors and appreciative guests and children safely at play. It is a vision that has withstood changes of time and trends and styles and even island-leveling hurricanes. It is a vision that has been handed down from generation to generation to generation and surely will continue to be handed down for as many years as one can see ahead.

The future may be uncertain, but the vision continues.

Thus far, Mayberry by the Sea endures.

Acknowledgments

As *with any book, those who deserve cred-it for their help on* Topsail Island: Mayberry by the Sea *are numerous.*

But there is no doubt who should be first. Allan Libby, president of the Greater Topsail Area Chamber of Commerce and Tourism, was instrumental every step of the way. Allan was among the first to contact me following my August 2005 column in the *Richmond Times-Dispatch* about visiting Topsail Island. He and I fleshed out the concept of a book during a barrage of e-mails. It was he who first mentioned the is-landers' own description, "Mayberry by the Sea." Along the way, he provided the unerring perspectives of both a cham-ber advocate and an objective critiquer, thanks in part to some early news training of his own. As my wife, Vicki, and I made several visits, Allan steered us toward the best and most knowledgeable interviewees and even made occasional lodg-ing accommodations. Finally, he made several research forays on my behalf, once notably driving the length of the island with a cell phone so we could correctly locate missile towers on a map. I thank him for all he did and for his friendship. Without Allan, this book would have taken twice as long and been only half as good—if indeed it existed at all.

I am also indebted to two distinctly different, if occasion-ally overlapping, groups of Topsailians.

First are the year-round residents. Evelyn Bradshaw in particular stands out. As a "come-here" who stayed, Evelyn knows the joy of Topsail. As one of the island's leading his-torical authorities, she knows the facts. And as a generous soul, she freely shared both. I could say the same of Barry Newsome, friendly and knowledgeable—and funny in that he continually downplayed his knowledge. Many other islanders were helpful, and for that I am grateful. Though I run the risk of inadvertently offending those I leave out, I feel I have to name a few. Among public officials, Garth Boyd, Zander Guy, Doug Medlin, Butch Parrish, Rodney Knowles, Loraine Carbone, Rickey Smith, Michael Halstead, and Daniel R. Salese III particularly stood out, as did Bill Godwin, Jeff Price, Greg Ludlum, Ed Lore, and Robin Orr among merchants.

The second group of islanders are the annual vacationers. I consider them an important part of Topsail not only for their numbers, which dwarf those of annual residents, but also for their passion for the island. Everyone I talked with gratefully shared stories. Many of their names are within these pages, and I hope that will suffice as thanks. Many other vacationers are not mentioned by name, but I thank them nonetheless.

I am also indebted to professional researchers, foremost among them Alan Watson, history professor of the University of North Carolina at Wilmington, who steered me to books on early coastal history when I was floundering. I also thank Kim Cumber of the State Archives of North Carolina, who found an old videotape; Jo Cooper and Marsha Hayes of the New Hanover County Library's North Carolina Room, who kept retrieving old news articles and patiently waited as I filled their copy machine with coins again and again; Mary Clark of The Library of Virginia, who helped me track down old North Carolina books in a different state; Aimee Boese of the Pender County Public Library, who made repeated trips to the files to find old articles when I visited and mailed me even more; and Rose Peters of the Missiles and More Museum in Topsail Beach, who was uncommonly gracious despite feeling trepidation over the release of some information. I should mention here the Wilmington, Jacksonville, Topsail, and Pender County newspapers. Being a newspaperman myself, I have always considered the so-called first drafts of history to be the most interesting and useful. Also, David Stallman's book on island history provided a road map; I ended up leaving the main road more often than not, but at least I knew where it was.

My gratitude extends to graphics artist Roy Wilhelm of the *Times-Dispatch* staff, who somehow created a unique and attractive map incorporating political markings, points of interest, and structures from a six-decades-old missile program. It is still the only one I've seen. For the book itself, I thank the good people of John F. Blair, Publisher: Carolyn Sakowski, president, who repeatedly went out of her way to help me and graciously kept whatever she really thought of my unending e-mail questions to herself; my editor, Steve Kirk, whose every recommendation showed a writer's care and improved the book; designer Sherry Roberts, who expertly crafted all this *stuff* into what you hold in your hands; and Ed Southern and Kim Byerly, for their help in sales and publicity, respectively. Every writer should be so fortunate as to work with people like these.

Finally, of course, I thank Vicki, who accompanied me and took pictures of everyone and everything. As with all of my life, she makes everything easier. But this time, she got some reward, at least. When my interviews ran long, she sometimes simply walked on over to the beach.

If there is insight provided in these pages, credit goes to all these and many other wonderful Topsailians. All errors of fact or perspective are mine.

References

Most information in this book comes from the author's observations and interviews.

Among the reference works consulted:

BOOKS

Barnes, Jay. *North Carolina's Hurricane History*. 3rd ed. Chapel Hill: University of North Carolina Press, 2001.

Beck, Ken, and Jim Clark. *The Andy Griffith Show Book*. New York: St. Martin's, 1985, 2000.

Butler, Lindley S. *Pirates, Privateers, and Rebel Raiders of the Carolina Coast*. Chapel Hill: University of North Carolina Press, 2000.

Lee, Robert E. *Blackbeard the Pirate: A Reappraisal of His Life and Times*. Winston-Salem, N.C.: John F. Blair, Publisher, 1974.

Milling, Chapman J. *Red Carolinians*. Chapel Hill: University of North Carolina Press, 1940.

Rankin, Hugh F. *The Pirates of Colonial North Carolina*. Raleigh: North Carolina Department of Cultural Resources, 1979.

Rights, Douglas L. *The American Indian in North Carolina*. Durham, N.C.: Duke University Press, 1947.

Sharpe, Bill. *A New Geography of North Carolina*. Vol. 3. 1961. Reprint, Raleigh, N.C.: Edwards & Broughton Company, 1966.

Stallman, David A. *Echoes of Topsail: Stories of the Island's Past*. 2nd ed. Sugarcreek, Ohio: Carlisle Printing, 2004.

Stick, David. *Graveyard of the Atlantic: Shipwrecks of the North Carolina Coast*. Chapel Hill: University of North Carolina Press, 1952.

Whitney, Phyllis A. *Amethyst Dreams*. New York: Crown Publishers, 1997.

MAGAZINES

Allen, Calvin H. "Living with Bears." *Wildlife in North Carolina* 62 (June 1998).

Allen, Joseph Baneth. "The Mystery Towers." *Journal of the Council on America's Past* (Summer 1991): 54-55.

———. "The Secret of Topsail Island." *The State* 53 (July 1985): 12-14.

———. "Towers of Topsail." *Encore Magazine* (September 18-24, 1986).

Brown, Dick. "The Topsail Island Secret: Operation 'Bumblebee.' " *Cape Fear Tidewater* 2 (March 1985) 6-8.

Cothran, B. J. "Waterline." *Topsail Magazine* 1 (Fall 2005): 10-12.

Grant, Lindsey. "The Mullet Fishermen," Part I. *The State* (May 1979): 8–11.

———. "The Mullet Fishermen," Part II, *The State* (July 1979): 16–17, 29.

Howell, Margaret S. "Business at the Breez-way: The Way They Were." *Cape Fear Tidewater* 2 (March 1985): 9-11.

"New Topsail Beach." *The State* 18 (May 26, 1951): 29.

Old Trudge. "The Fishingest Island." *The State* 35 (June 1, 1967): 26-27.

Smith, Scott. "Time Warp." *The State* 62 (March 1995): 30-32.

Smith, Sue Medlin. "Topsail Island: Then and Now." *Carolina Homes & Interiors* (Spring 2006): 20-23, 25-26.

Turnage, Sheila. "Operation Bumblebee." *The State* 62 (March 1995): 33-36.

Venters, Vic. "Bears in the East." *Wildlife in North Carolina* 60 (January 1996): 5-11.

NEWSPAPERS

Bill Reaves Collection (of newspaper clippings), 1868-1941. New Hanover County Public Library and Pender County Public Library.

Coastal Carolinian. 1989-90.

Jacksonville Daily News. 2006.

Pender Chronicle. 1953, 1955, 1965, 1979, 1987.

Pender Post. 2005-6.

Pender Sounds. 1989-90.

Topsail Advertiser. 1995, 2005-6.

Topsail Voice. 2005-6.

Wallace Enterprise. 1987.

Wilmington News. 1939.

Wilmington Star/Morning Star/Star-News. 1954, 1965-66, 1970, 1973-74, 1985-97, 2005.

MISCELLANEOUS

Coaster: Topsail Guide to the Treasure Coast. Morehead City: N.C. Coast Communications.

Topsail Area Guide. Surf City, N.C.: Greater Topsail Chamber of Commerce.

Index

Algonquin Indians, 10
Allen, Joseph Baneth, 46
Amethyst Dreams, 32-33
Anderson Boulevard, 82, 139, 158, 161
Anderson, J. G., 52, 82-84
Anderson, J. G. Jr., 82-83
Andy Griffith Show, The, 4-5, 151, 152, 153, 154-55, 160
Arnold, Patty, 93
Assembly Building, *37*, 38, 39, 40, 47. *See also* Operation Bumblebee; Missiles and More Museum
Atlantic Beach, N.C., 66
Atlantis Restaurant, 118
Autumn With Topsail festival, 86-87, 89, 178

Barnacle Bill's Pier and Restaurant, 50, 97, 98, 100
Barnes, Jay, 66, 71-72, 74-75, 77
Barwick Avenue, 161
Barwick, Hugh, Sr., 57
Bath, N.C., 14, 17
Batson, Travis James, 10
Batts' Grill, 98, 100, *101*
Batts, J. B., 98, 99
Batts, James, 98
Batts, Kenny, 98
Batts, Roland, 98
"beach glass," 169
Beach House Marina, 95, *103*, 193
beach replenishment, 114, 121, *123*, 147, 175, *206*, 209-10
Beach Shop and Grill, 4, 81-82, 85-86, 130, 205, 207

bear at Topsail Beach, 157-64, *159*, *160*
Beasley, Jean, 177-86, *183*
Beasley, Karen, 177, 181
Beaufort Inlet, 17, 18
Beaufort, N.C., 18, 190
Becker, Caste, 168
Becker, Don, 167, 168
Bedford, Julie, 168
Blackbeard, 12-18, *15*, 23, 27, 28, 30, 161
Blake, Frank, 171-72
Blake, Quinn, 171-72
Bland, Bill, 87
Bland property, 28
Blossom, Lynia, 94
Blue Gecko, 82
Bonnet, Stede, 12-13, 17
Boryk, M. A., 202-3
Boxcar Willie, 62
Boyd, Garth, 5-8, 203, 208
Boyd, Lynette, 5-6
Bradshaw, Evelyn, 16-17, 31-32, 51, 127-29, *128*
Bradshaw, Hoyt, *128*, 129
Bradshaw, W. J., 161
Bradt, Inez, 209
Brashear, Mary, 121-24
Brashear, Rusty, 121-24
Breezeway Motel and Restaurant, 69, 83, 126, 130, 145, 166
Breez-way Inn and Café. *See* Breezeway Motel and Restaurant
Bridges, Robert, 173-74
Brigantine, N.J., 180
Broadhurst, Cecile Mayrand, 28

221